The Tempest

By Edward de Vere

Art:
Portrait of Edward de Vere
17th Earl of Oxford (1550-1604)

This edition produced by
Verus Publishing

V | P

www.verusbooks.com

ISBN:978-1-951267-30-8
Imprint / Publisher: Verus Publishing

The Author

Edward de Vere, 17th Earl of Oxford

Biography and Bibliography
After the Play

A Preverse

Drone on ye learned scholars of the day
As to with whom the words ahead the credit lay.
For our part though can be no further doubt
That the author of these words has been found out
To be a person lordly and refined
On whom the light of wit so boldly shined
That to keep this wit from tearing in the fray
He gave another, lesser wit his say.

Now let the least of wits
That writes these paltry lines
Yield to him whose peerless name
Should be with reverence spake.
Let this name be not of history's misassigns
Whose pen and verse have made the earth to shake.

The Tempest

By Edward de Vere

The Main Characters

Prospero – Duke of Milan

Miranda – Daughter of Prospero

Ariel – Spirit in Prospero's service

Caliban –A savage monster and Servent of Prospero

Alonso – King of Naples

Sebastian – Alonso's brother

Antonio – Prospero's brother and the usurping Duke of Milan

Ferdinand – Alonso's son

Gonzalo – An old and honest Counselor

Adrian – Lord serving under Alonso

Francisco – Lord serving under Alonso

Trinculo – The King's jester

Stephano – Drunken butler to the King

Juno – Roman Goddess of marriage

ACT I

SCENE I.

On a ship at sea: a tempestuous noise

of thunder and lightning heard.

Enter a Master and a Boatswain

Master
Boatswain!
Boatswain
Here, master: what cheer?
Master
Good, speak to the mariners: fall to't, yarely,
or we run ourselves aground: bestir, bestir.

Exit

Enter Mariners

Boatswain
Heigh, my hearts! cheerly, cheerly, my hearts!
yare, yare! Take in the topsail. Tend to the
master's whistle. Blow, till thou burst thy wind,
if room enough!

Enter ALONSO, SEBASTIAN, ANTONIO, FERDINAND,
GONZALO, and others

ALONSO
Good boatswain, have care. Where's the master?
Play the men.
Boatswain

5

I pray now, keep below.
ANTONIO
Where is the master, boatswain?
Boatswain
Do you not hear him? You mar our labour: keep your
cabins: you do assist the storm.
GONZALO
Nay, good, be patient.
Boatswain
When the sea is. Hence! What cares these roarers
for the name of king? To cabin: silence! trouble us not.
GONZALO
Good, yet remember whom thou hast aboard.
Boatswain
None that I more love than myself. You are a
counsellor; if you can command these elements to
silence, and work the peace of the present, we will
not hand a rope more; use your authority: if you
cannot, give thanks you have lived so long, and make
yourself ready in your cabin for the mischance of
the hour, if it so hap. Cheerly, good hearts! Out
of our way, I say.

Exit

GONZALO
I have great comfort from this fellow: methinks he
hath no drowning mark upon him; his complexion is
perfect gallows. Stand fast, good Fate, to his
hanging: make the rope of his destiny our cable,
for our own doth little advantage. If he be not
born to be hanged, our case is miserable.

Exeunt

Re-enter Boatswain

Boatswain
　Down with the topmast! yare! lower, lower! Bring
　her to try with main-course.

A cry within

　A plague upon this howling! they are louder than
　the weather or our office.

Re-enter SEBASTIAN, ANTONIO, and GONZALO

　Yet again! what do you here? Shall we give o'er
　and drown? Have you a mind to sink?
SEBASTIAN
　A pox o' your throat, you bawling, blasphemous,
　incharitable dog!
Boatswain
　Work you then.
ANTONIO
　Hang, cur! hang, you whoreson, insolent noisemaker!
　We are less afraid to be drowned than thou art.
GONZALO
　I'll warrant him for drowning; though the ship were
　no stronger than a nutshell and as leaky as an
　unstanched wench.
Boatswain
　Lay her a-hold, a-hold! set her two courses off to
　sea again; lay her off.

Enter Mariners wet

Mariners
　All lost! to prayers, to prayers! all lost!
Boatswain

What, must our mouths be cold?
GONZALO
The king and prince at prayers! let's assist them,
For our case is as theirs.
SEBASTIAN
I'm out of patience.
ANTONIO
We are merely cheated of our lives by drunkards:
This wide-chapp'd rascal--would thou mightst lie
drowning
The washing of ten tides!
GONZALO
He'll be hang'd yet,
Though every drop of water swear against it
And gape at widest to glut him.
A confused noise within: 'Mercy on us!'-- 'We split, we
split!'--'Farewell, my wife and children!'-- 'Farewell,
brother!'--'We split, we split, we split!'
ANTONIO
Let's all sink with the king.
SEBASTIAN
Let's take leave of him.

Exeunt ANTONIO and SEBASTIAN

GONZALO
Now would I give a thousand furlongs of sea for an
acre of barren ground, long heath, brown furze, any
thing. The wills above be done! but I would fain
die a dry death.

Exeunt

SCENE *II.*

The island. Before PROSPERO'S cell.

Enter PROSPERO and MIRANDA

MIRANDA
  If by your art, my dearest father, you have
  Put the wild waters in this roar, allay them.
  The sky, it seems, would pour down stinking pitch,
  But that the sea, mounting to the welkin's cheek,
  Dashes the fire out. O, I have suffered
  With those that I saw suffer: a brave vessel,
  Who had, no doubt, some noble creature in her,
  Dash'd all to pieces. O, the cry did knock
  Against my very heart. Poor souls, they perish'd.
  Had I been any god of power, I would
  Have sunk the sea within the earth or ere
  It should the good ship so have swallow'd and
  The fraughting souls within her.
PROSPERO
  Be collected:
  No more amazement: tell your piteous heart
  There's no harm done.
MIRANDA
  O, woe the day!
PROSPERO
  No harm.
  I have done nothing but in care of thee,
  Of thee, my dear one, thee, my daughter, who
  Art ignorant of what thou art, nought knowing
  Of whence I am, nor that I am more better
  Than Prospero, master of a full poor cell,
  And thy no greater father.
MIRANDA
  More to know

Did never meddle with my thoughts.
PROSPERO
  'Tis time
  I should inform thee farther. Lend thy hand,
  And pluck my magic garment from me. So:

  Lays down his mantle

  Lie there, my art. Wipe thou thine eyes; have comfort.
  The direful spectacle of the wreck, which touch'd
  The very virtue of compassion in thee,
  I have with such provision in mine art
  So safely ordered that there is no soul--
  No, not so much perdition as an hair
  Betid to any creature in the vessel
  Which thou heard'st cry, which thou saw'st sink. Sit
  down;
  For thou must now know farther.
MIRANDA
  You have often
  Begun to tell me what I am, but stopp'd
  And left me to a bootless inquisition,
  Concluding 'Stay: not yet.'
PROSPERO
  The hour's now come;
  The very minute bids thee ope thine ear;
  Obey and be attentive. Canst thou remember
  A time before we came unto this cell?
  I do not think thou canst, for then thou wast not
  Out three years old.
MIRANDA
  Certainly, sir, I can.
PROSPERO
  By what? by any other house or person?
  Of any thing the image tell me that

Hath kept with thy remembrance.
MIRANDA
    'Tis far off
    And rather like a dream than an assurance
    That my remembrance warrants. Had I not
    Four or five women once that tended me?
PROSPERO
    Thou hadst, and more, Miranda. But how is it
    That this lives in thy mind? What seest thou else
    In the dark backward and abysm of time?
    If thou remember'st aught ere thou camest here,
    How thou camest here thou mayst.
MIRANDA
    But that I do not.
PROSPERO
    Twelve year since, Miranda, twelve year since,
    Thy father was the Duke of Milan and
    A prince of power.
MIRANDA
    Sir, are not you my father?
PROSPERO
    Thy mother was a piece of virtue, and
    She said thou wast my daughter; and thy father
    Was Duke of Milan; and thou his only heir
    And princess no worse issued.
MIRANDA
    O the heavens!
    What foul play had we, that we came from thence?
    Or blessed was't we did?
PROSPERO
    Both, both, my girl:
    By foul play, as thou say'st, were we heaved thence,
    But blessedly holp hither.
MIRANDA

O, my heart bleeds
To think o' the teen that I have turn'd you to,
Which is from my remembrance! Please you, farther.

PROSPERO

My brother and thy uncle, call'd Antonio--
I pray thee, mark me--that a brother should
Be so perfidious!--he whom next thyself
Of all the world I loved and to him put
The manage of my state; as at that time
Through all the signories it was the first
And Prospero the prime duke, being so reputed
In dignity, and for the liberal arts
Without a parallel; those being all my study,
The government I cast upon my brother
And to my state grew stranger, being transported
And rapt in secret studies. Thy false uncle--
Dost thou attend me?

MIRANDA

Sir, most heedfully.

PROSPERO

Being once perfected how to grant suits,
How to deny them, who to advance and who
To trash for over-topping, new created
The creatures that were mine, I say, or changed 'em,
Or else new form'd 'em; having both the key
Of officer and office, set all hearts i' the state
To what tune pleased his ear; that now he was
The ivy which had hid my princely trunk,
And suck'd my verdure out on't. Thou attend'st not.

MIRANDA

O, good sir, I do.

PROSPERO

I pray thee, mark me.
I, thus neglecting worldly ends, all dedicated

To closeness and the bettering of my mind
With that which, but by being so retired,
O'er-prized all popular rate, in my false brother
Awaked an evil nature; and my trust,
Like a good parent, did beget of him
A falsehood in its contrary as great
As my trust was; which had indeed no limit,
A confidence sans bound. He being thus lorded,
Not only with what my revenue yielded,
But what my power might else exact, like one
Who having into truth, by telling of it,
Made such a sinner of his memory,
To credit his own lie, he did believe
He was indeed the duke; out o' the substitution
And executing the outward face of royalty,
With all prerogative: hence his ambition growing--
Dost thou hear?

MIRANDA
    Your tale, sir, would cure deafness.

PROSPERO
    To have no screen between this part he play'd
And him he play'd it for, he needs will be
Absolute Milan. Me, poor man, my library
Was dukedom large enough: of temporal royalties
He thinks me now incapable; confederates--
So dry he was for sway--wi' the King of Naples
To give him annual tribute, do him homage,
Subject his coronet to his crown and bend
The dukedom yet unbow'd--alas, poor Milan!--
To most ignoble stooping.

MIRANDA
    O the heavens!

PROSPERO
    Mark his condition and the event; then tell me

If this might be a brother.
MIRANDA
I should sin
To think but nobly of my grandmother:
Good wombs have borne bad sons.
PROSPERO
Now the condition.
The King of Naples, being an enemy
To me inveterate, hearkens my brother's suit;
Which was, that he, in lieu o' the premises
Of homage and I know not how much tribute,
Should presently extirpate me and mine
Out of the dukedom and confer fair Milan
With all the honours on my brother: whereon,
A treacherous army levied, one midnight
Fated to the purpose did Antonio open
The gates of Milan, and, i' the dead of darkness,
The ministers for the purpose hurried thence
Me and thy crying self.
MIRANDA
Alack, for pity!
I, not remembering how I cried out then,
Will cry it o'er again: it is a hint
That wrings mine eyes to't.
PROSPERO
Hear a little further
And then I'll bring thee to the present business
Which now's upon's; without the which this story
Were most impertinent.
MIRANDA
Wherefore did they not
That hour destroy us?
PROSPERO
Well demanded, wench:

My tale provokes that question. Dear, they durst not,
So dear the love my people bore me, nor set
A mark so bloody on the business, but
With colours fairer painted their foul ends.
In few, they hurried us aboard a bark,
Bore us some leagues to sea; where they prepared
A rotten carcass of a boat, not rigg'd,
Nor tackle, sail, nor mast; the very rats
Instinctively had quit it: there they hoist us,
To cry to the sea that roar'd to us, to sigh
To the winds whose pity, sighing back again,
Did us but loving wrong.

MIRANDA

Alack, what trouble
Was I then to you!

PROSPERO

O, a cherubim
Thou wast that did preserve me. Thou didst smile.
Infused with a fortitude from heaven,
When I have deck'd the sea with drops full salt,
Under my burthen groan'd; which raised in me
An undergoing stomach, to bear up
Against what should ensue.

MIRANDA

How came we ashore?

PROSPERO

By Providence divine.
Some food we had and some fresh water that
A noble Neapolitan, Gonzalo,
Out of his charity, being then appointed
Master of this design, did give us, with
Rich garments, linens, stuffs and necessaries,
Which since have steaded much; so, of his gentleness,
Knowing I loved my books, he furnish'd me

From mine own library with volumes that
I prize above my dukedom.
MIRANDA
Would I might
But ever see that man!
PROSPERO
Now I arise:

Resumes his mantle

Sit still, and hear the last of our sea-sorrow.
Here in this island we arrived; and here
Have I, thy schoolmaster, made thee more profit
Than other princesses can that have more time
For vainer hours and tutors not so careful.
MIRANDA
Heavens thank you for't! And now, I pray you, sir,
For still 'tis beating in my mind, your reason
For raising this sea-storm?
PROSPERO
Know thus far forth.
By accident most strange, bountiful Fortune,
Now my dear lady, hath mine enemies
Brought to this shore; and by my prescience
I find my zenith doth depend upon
A most auspicious star, whose influence
If now I court not but omit, my fortunes
Will ever after droop. Here cease more questions:
Thou art inclined to sleep; 'tis a good dulness,
And give it way: I know thou canst not choose.

MIRANDA sleeps

Come away, servant, come. I am ready now.
Approach, my Ariel, come.

Enter ARIEL

ARIEL

    All hail, great master! grave sir, hail! I come
    To answer thy best pleasure; be't to fly,
    To swim, to dive into the fire, to ride
    On the curl'd clouds, to thy strong bidding task
    Ariel and all his quality.

PROSPERO

    Hast thou, spirit,
    Perform'd to point the tempest that I bade thee?

ARIEL

    To every article.
    I boarded the king's ship; now on the beak,
    Now in the waist, the deck, in every cabin,
    I flamed amazement: sometime I'ld divide,
    And burn in many places; on the topmast,
    The yards and bowsprit, would I flame distinctly,
    Then meet and join. Jove's lightnings, the precursors
    O' the dreadful thunder-claps, more momentary
    And sight-outrunning were not; the fire and cracks
    Of sulphurous roaring the most mighty Neptune
    Seem to besiege and make his bold waves tremble,
    Yea, his dread trident shake.

PROSPERO

    My brave spirit!
    Who was so firm, so constant, that this coil
    Would not infect his reason?

ARIEL

    Not a soul
    But felt a fever of the mad and play'd
    Some tricks of desperation. All but mariners
    Plunged in the foaming brine and quit the vessel,
    Then all afire with me: the king's son, Ferdinand,

With hair up-staring,--then like reeds, not hair,--
Was the first man that leap'd; cried, 'Hell is empty
And all the devils are here.'
PROSPERO
Why that's my spirit!
But was not this nigh shore?
ARIEL
Close by, my master.
PROSPERO
But are they, Ariel, safe?
ARIEL
Not a hair perish'd;
On their sustaining garments not a blemish,
But fresher than before: and, as thou badest me,
In troops I have dispersed them 'bout the isle.
The king's son have I landed by himself;
Whom I left cooling of the air with sighs
In an odd angle of the isle and sitting,
His arms in this sad knot.
PROSPERO
Of the king's ship
The mariners say how thou hast disposed
And all the rest o' the fleet.
ARIEL
Safely in harbour
Is the king's ship; in the deep nook, where once
Thou call'dst me up at midnight to fetch dew
From the still-vex'd Bermoothes, there she's hid:
The mariners all under hatches stow'd;
Who, with a charm join'd to their suffer'd labour,
I have left asleep; and for the rest o' the fleet
Which I dispersed, they all have met again
And are upon the Mediterranean flote,
Bound sadly home for Naples,

Supposing that they saw the king's ship wreck'd
And his great person perish.
PROSPERO
Ariel, thy charge
Exactly is perform'd: but there's more work.
What is the time o' the day?
ARIEL
Past the mid season.
PROSPERO
At least two glasses. The time 'twixt six and now
Must by us both be spent most preciously.
ARIEL
Is there more toil? Since thou dost give me pains,
Let me remember thee what thou hast promised,
Which is not yet perform'd me.
PROSPERO
How now? moody?
What is't thou canst demand?
ARIEL
My liberty.
PROSPERO
Before the time be out? no more!
ARIEL
I prithee,
Remember I have done thee worthy service;
Told thee no lies, made thee no mistakings, served
Without or grudge or grumblings: thou didst promise
To bate me a full year.
PROSPERO
Dost thou forget
From what a torment I did free thee?
ARIEL
No.
PROSPERO

Thou dost, and think'st it much to tread the ooze
Of the salt deep,
To run upon the sharp wind of the north,
To do me business in the veins o' the earth
When it is baked with frost.

ARIEL

I do not, sir.

PROSPERO

Thou liest, malignant thing! Hast thou forgot
The foul witch Sycorax, who with age and envy
Was grown into a hoop? hast thou forgot her?

ARIEL

No, sir.

PROSPERO

Thou hast. Where was she born? speak; tell me.

ARIEL

Sir, in Argier.

PROSPERO

O, was she so? I must
Once in a month recount what thou hast been,
Which thou forget'st. This damn'd witch Sycorax,
For mischiefs manifold and sorceries terrible
To enter human hearing, from Argier,
Thou know'st, was banish'd: for one thing she did
They would not take her life. Is not this true?

ARIEL

Ay, sir.

PROSPERO

This blue-eyed hag was hither brought with child
And here was left by the sailors. Thou, my slave,
As thou report'st thyself, wast then her servant;
And, for thou wast a spirit too delicate
To act her earthy and abhorr'd commands,
Refusing her grand hests, she did confine thee,

By help of her more potent ministers
And in her most unmitigable rage,
Into a cloven pine; within which rift
Imprison'd thou didst painfully remain
A dozen years; within which space she died
And left thee there; where thou didst vent thy groans
As fast as mill-wheels strike. Then was this island--
Save for the son that she did litter here,
A freckled whelp hag-born--not honour'd with
A human shape.

ARIEL

Yes, Caliban her son.

PROSPERO

Dull thing, I say so; he, that Caliban
Whom now I keep in service. Thou best know'st
What torment I did find thee in; thy groans
Did make wolves howl and penetrate the breasts
Of ever angry bears: it was a torment
To lay upon the damn'd, which Sycorax
Could not again undo: it was mine art,
When I arrived and heard thee, that made gape
The pine and let thee out.

ARIEL

I thank thee, master.

PROSPERO

If thou more murmur'st, I will rend an oak
And peg thee in his knotty entrails till
Thou hast howl'd away twelve winters.

ARIEL

Pardon, master;
I will be correspondent to command
And do my spiriting gently.

PROSPERO

Do so, and after two days

I will discharge thee.
ARIEL
That's my noble master!
What shall I do? say what; what shall I do?
PROSPERO
Go make thyself like a nymph o' the sea: be subject
To no sight but thine and mine, invisible
To every eyeball else. Go take this shape
And hither come in't: go, hence with diligence!

Exit ARIEL

Awake, dear heart, awake! thou hast slept well; Awake!
MIRANDA
The strangeness of your story put
Heaviness in me.
PROSPERO
Shake it off. Come on;
We'll visit Caliban my slave, who never
Yields us kind answer.
MIRANDA
'Tis a villain, sir,
I do not love to look on.
PROSPERO
But, as 'tis,
We cannot miss him: he does make our fire,
Fetch in our wood and serves in offices
That profit us. What, ho! slave! Caliban!
Thou earth, thou! speak.
CALIBAN
[Within] There's wood enough within.
PROSPERO
Come forth, I say! there's other business for thee:
Come, thou tortoise! when?

Re-enter ARIEL like a water-nymph

Fine apparition! My quaint Ariel,
Hark in thine ear.
ARIEL
My lord it shall be done.

Exit

PROSPERO
Thou poisonous slave, got by the devil himself
Upon thy wicked dam, come forth!

Enter CALIBAN

CALIBAN
As wicked dew as e'er my mother brush'd
With raven's feather from unwholesome fen
Drop on you both! a south-west blow on ye
And blister you all o'er!
PROSPERO
For this, be sure, to-night thou shalt have cramps,
Side-stitches that shall pen thy breath up; urchins
Shall, for that vast of night that they may work,
All exercise on thee; thou shalt be pinch'd
As thick as honeycomb, each pinch more stinging
Than bees that made 'em.
CALIBAN
I must eat my dinner.
This island's mine, by Sycorax my mother,
Which thou takest from me. When thou camest first,
Thou strokedst me and madest much of me, wouldst
give me
Water with berries in't, and teach me how
To name the bigger light, and how the less,

That burn by day and night: and then I loved thee
And show'd thee all the qualities o' the isle,
The fresh springs, brine-pits, barren place and fertile:
Cursed be I that did so! All the charms
Of Sycorax, toads, beetles, bats, light on you!
For I am all the subjects that you have,
Which first was mine own king: and here you sty me
In this hard rock, whiles you do keep from me
The rest o' the island.

PROSPERO

Thou most lying slave,
Whom stripes may move, not kindness! I have used
thee,
Filth as thou art, with human care, and lodged thee
In mine own cell, till thou didst seek to violate
The honour of my child.

CALIBAN

O ho, O ho! would't had been done!
Thou didst prevent me; I had peopled else
This isle with Calibans.

PROSPERO

Abhorred slave,
Which any print of goodness wilt not take,
Being capable of all ill! I pitied thee,
Took pains to make thee speak, taught thee each hour
One thing or other: when thou didst not, savage,
Know thine own meaning, but wouldst gabble like
A thing most brutish, I endow'd thy purposes
With words that made them known. But thy vile race,
Though thou didst learn, had that in't which
good natures
Could not abide to be with; therefore wast thou
Deservedly confined into this rock,
Who hadst deserved more than a prison.

CALIBAN
  You taught me language; and my profit on't
  Is, I know how to curse. The red plague rid you
  For learning me your language!
PROSPERO
  Hag-seed, hence!
  Fetch us in fuel; and be quick, thou'rt best,
  To answer other business. Shrug'st thou, malice?
  If thou neglect'st or dost unwillingly
  What I command, I'll rack thee with old cramps,
  Fill all thy bones with aches, make thee roar
  That beasts shall tremble at thy din.
CALIBAN
  No, pray thee.

Aside

  I must obey: his art is of such power,
  It would control my dam's god, Setebos,
  and make a vassal of him.
PROSPERO
  So, slave; hence!

Exit CALIBAN

Re-enter ARIEL, invisible, playing and singing;
FERDINAND following

ARIEL'S song.
  Come unto these yellow sands,
  And then take hands:
  Courtsied when you have and kiss'd
  The wild waves whist,
  Foot it featly here and there;
  And, sweet sprites, the burthen bear.

Hark, hark!

Burthen [dispersedly, within]

The watch-dogs bark!
Burthen Bow-wow

Hark, hark! I hear
The strain of strutting chanticleer
Cry, Cock-a-diddle-dow.
FERDINAND
Where should this music be? i' the air or the earth?
It sounds no more: and sure, it waits upon
Some god o' the island. Sitting on a bank,
Weeping again the king my father's wreck,
This music crept by me upon the waters,
Allaying both their fury and my passion
With its sweet air: thence I have follow'd it,
Or it hath drawn me rather. But 'tis gone.
No, it begins again.

ARIEL sings

Full fathom five thy father lies;
Of his bones are coral made;
Those are pearls that were his eyes:
Nothing of him that doth fade
But doth suffer a sea-change
Into something rich and strange.
Sea-nymphs hourly ring his knell

Burthen Ding-dong

Hark! now I hear them,--Ding-dong, bell.
FERDINAND
The ditty does remember my drown'd father.

This is no mortal business, nor no sound
That the earth owes. I hear it now above me.
PROSPERO
The fringed curtains of thine eye advance
And say what thou seest yond.
MIRANDA
What is't? a spirit?
Lord, how it looks about! Believe me, sir,
It carries a brave form. But 'tis a spirit.
PROSPERO
No, wench; it eats and sleeps and hath such senses
As we have, such. This gallant which thou seest
Was in the wreck; and, but he's something stain'd
With grief that's beauty's canker, thou mightst call him
A goodly person: he hath lost his fellows
And strays about to find 'em.
MIRANDA
I might call him
A thing divine, for nothing natural
I ever saw so noble.
PROSPERO
[Aside] It goes on, I see,
As my soul prompts it. Spirit, fine spirit! I'll free thee
Within two days for this.
FERDINAND
Most sure, the goddess
On whom these airs attend! Vouchsafe my prayer
May know if you remain upon this island;
And that you will some good instruction give
How I may bear me here: my prime request,
Which I do last pronounce, is, O you wonder!
If you be maid or no?
MIRANDA
No wonder, sir;

But certainly a maid.
FERDINAND
　　My language! heavens!
　　I am the best of them that speak this speech,
　　Were I but where 'tis spoken.
PROSPERO
　　How? the best?
　　What wert thou, if the King of Naples heard thee?
FERDINAND
　　A single thing, as I am now, that wonders
　　To hear thee speak of Naples. He does hear me;
　　And that he does I weep: myself am Naples,
　　Who with mine eyes, never since at ebb, beheld
　　The king my father wreck'd.
MIRANDA
　　Alack, for mercy!
FERDINAND
　　Yes, faith, and all his lords; the Duke of Milan
　　And his brave son being twain.
PROSPERO
　　[Aside]　　　　The Duke of Milan
　　And his more braver daughter could control thee,
　　If now 'twere fit to do't. At the first sight
　　They have changed eyes. Delicate Ariel,
　　I'll set thee free for this.

To FERDINAND

　　A word, good sir;
　　I fear you have done yourself some wrong: a word.
MIRANDA
　　Why speaks my father so ungently? This
　　Is the third man that e'er I saw, the first
　　That e'er I sigh'd for: pity move my father
　　To be inclined my way!

FERDINAND
  O, if a virgin,
  And your affection not gone forth, I'll make you
  The queen of Naples.
PROSPERO
  Soft, sir! one word more.

Aside

  They are both in either's powers; but this swift business
  I must uneasy make, lest too light winning
  Make the prize light.

To FERDINAND

  One word more; I charge thee
  That thou attend me: thou dost here usurp
  The name thou owest not; and hast put thyself
  Upon this island as a spy, to win it
  From me, the lord on't.
FERDINAND
  No, as I am a man.
MIRANDA
  There's nothing ill can dwell in such a temple:
  If the ill spirit have so fair a house,
  Good things will strive to dwell with't.
PROSPERO
  Follow me.
  Speak not you for him; he's a traitor. Come;
  I'll manacle thy neck and feet together:
  Sea-water shalt thou drink; thy food shall be
  The fresh-brook muscles, wither'd roots and husks
  Wherein the acorn cradled. Follow.
FERDINAND
  No;

I will resist such entertainment till
Mine enemy has more power.

Draws, and is charmed from moving

MIRANDA
O dear father,
Make not too rash a trial of him, for
He's gentle and not fearful.
PROSPERO
What? I say,
My foot my tutor? Put thy sword up, traitor;
Who makest a show but darest not strike, thy conscience
Is so possess'd with guilt: come from thy ward,
For I can here disarm thee with this stick
And make thy weapon drop.
MIRANDA
Beseech you, father.
PROSPERO
Hence! hang not on my garments.
MIRANDA
Sir, have pity;
I'll be his surety.
PROSPERO
Silence! one word more
Shall make me chide thee, if not hate thee. What!
An advocate for an imposter! hush!
Thou think'st there is no more such shapes as he,
Having seen but him and Caliban: foolish wench!
To the most of men this is a Caliban
And they to him are angels.
MIRANDA
My affections
Are then most humble; I have no ambition
To see a goodlier man.

PROSPERO
    Come on; obey:
    Thy nerves are in their infancy again
    And have no vigour in them.
FERDINAND
    So they are;
    My spirits, as in a dream, are all bound up.
    My father's loss, the weakness which I feel,
    The wreck of all my friends, nor this man's threats,
    To whom I am subdued, are but light to me,
    Might I but through my prison once a day
    Behold this maid: all corners else o' the earth
    Let liberty make use of; space enough
    Have I in such a prison.
PROSPERO
    [Aside] It works.

To FERDINAND

Come on.
Thou hast done well, fine Ariel!

To FERDINAND

Follow me.

To ARIEL

Hark what thou else shalt do me.
MIRANDA
    Be of comfort;
    My father's of a better nature, sir,
    Than he appears by speech: this is unwonted
    Which now came from him.
PROSPERO
    Thou shalt be free

As mountain winds: but then exactly do
All points of my command.

ARIEL

To the syllable.

PROSPERO

Come, follow. Speak not for him.

Exeunt

ACT II

SCENE I.

Another part of the island.

*Enter ALONSO, SEBASTIAN, ANTONIO, GONZALO,
ADRIAN, FRANCISCO, and others*

GONZALO
Beseech you, sir, be merry; you have cause,
So have we all, of joy; for our escape
Is much beyond our loss. Our hint of woe
Is common; every day some sailor's wife,
The masters of some merchant and the merchant
Have just our theme of woe; but for the miracle,
I mean our preservation, few in millions
Can speak like us: then wisely, good sir, weigh
Our sorrow with our comfort.

ALONSO
Prithee, peace.

SEBASTIAN
He receives comfort like cold porridge.

ANTONIO
The visitor will not give him o'er so.

SEBASTIAN
Look he's winding up the watch of his wit;
by and by it will strike.

GONZALO
Sir,--

SEBASTIAN
One: tell.

GONZALO
When every grief is entertain'd that's offer'd,
Comes to the entertainer--

SEBASTIAN
A dollar.
GONZALO
Dolour comes to him, indeed: you
have spoken truer than you purposed.
SEBASTIAN
You have taken it wiselier than I meant you should.
GONZALO
Therefore, my lord,--
ANTONIO
Fie, what a spendthrift is he of his tongue!
ALONSO
I prithee, spare.
GONZALO
Well, I have done: but yet,--
SEBASTIAN
He will be talking.
ANTONIO
Which, of he or Adrian, for a good
wager, first begins to crow?
SEBASTIAN
The old cock.
ANTONIO
The cockerel.
SEBASTIAN
Done. The wager?
ANTONIO
A laughter.
SEBASTIAN
A match!
ADRIAN
Though this island seem to be desert,--
SEBASTIAN
Ha, ha, ha! So, you're paid.

ADRIAN
Uninhabitable and almost inaccessible,--
SEBASTIAN
Yet,--
ADRIAN
Yet,--
ANTONIO
He could not miss't.
ADRIAN
It must needs be of subtle, tender and delicate
temperance.
ANTONIO
Temperance was a delicate wench.
SEBASTIAN
Ay, and a subtle; as he most learnedly delivered.
ADRIAN
The air breathes upon us here most sweetly.
SEBASTIAN
As if it had lungs and rotten ones.
ANTONIO
Or as 'twere perfumed by a fen.
GONZALO
Here is everything advantageous to life.
ANTONIO
True; save means to live.
SEBASTIAN
Of that there's none, or little.
GONZALO
How lush and lusty the grass looks! how green!
ANTONIO
The ground indeed is tawny.
SEBASTIAN
With an eye of green in't.
ANTONIO

He misses not much.

SEBASTIAN

No; he doth but mistake the truth totally.

GONZALO

But the rarity of it is,--which is indeed almost
beyond credit,--

SEBASTIAN

As many vouched rarities are.

GONZALO

That our garments, being, as they were, drenched in
the sea, hold notwithstanding their freshness and
glosses, being rather new-dyed than stained with
salt water.

ANTONIO

If but one of his pockets could speak, would it not
say he lies?

SEBASTIAN

Ay, or very falsely pocket up his report

GONZALO

Methinks our garments are now as fresh as when we
put them on first in Afric, at the marriage of
the king's fair daughter Claribel to the King of Tunis.

SEBASTIAN

'Twas a sweet marriage, and we prosper well in our
return.

ADRIAN

Tunis was never graced before with such a paragon to
their queen.

GONZALO

Not since widow Dido's time.

ANTONIO

Widow! a pox o' that! How came that widow in?
widow Dido!

SEBASTIAN

What if he had said 'widower AEneas' too? Good Lord,
how you take it!

ADRIAN

'Widow Dido' said you? you make me study of that:
she was of Carthage, not of Tunis.

GONZALO

This Tunis, sir, was Carthage.

ADRIAN

Carthage?

GONZALO

I assure you, Carthage.

SEBASTIAN

His word is more than the miraculous harp; he hath
raised the wall and houses too.

ANTONIO

What impossible matter will he make easy next?

SEBASTIAN

I think he will carry this island home in his pocket
and give it his son for an apple.

ANTONIO

And, sowing the kernels of it in the sea, bring
forth more islands.

GONZALO

Ay.

ANTONIO

Why, in good time.

GONZALO

Sir, we were talking that our garments seem now
as fresh as when we were at Tunis at the marriage
of your daughter, who is now queen.

ANTONIO

And the rarest that e'er came there.

SEBASTIAN

Bate, I beseech you, widow Dido.

ANTONIO
  O, widow Dido! ay, widow Dido.
GONZALO
  Is not, sir, my doublet as fresh as the first day I
  wore it? I mean, in a sort.
ANTONIO
  That sort was well fished for.
GONZALO
  When I wore it at your daughter's marriage?
ALONSO
  You cram these words into mine ears against
  The stomach of my sense. Would I had never
  Married my daughter there! for, coming thence,
  My son is lost and, in my rate, she too,
  Who is so far from Italy removed
  I ne'er again shall see her. O thou mine heir
  Of Naples and of Milan, what strange fish
  Hath made his meal on thee?
FRANCISCO
  Sir, he may live:
  I saw him beat the surges under him,
  And ride upon their backs; he trod the water,
  Whose enmity he flung aside, and breasted
  The surge most swoln that met him; his bold head
  'Bove the contentious waves he kept, and oar'd
  Himself with his good arms in lusty stroke
  To the shore, that o'er his wave-worn basis bow'd,
  As stooping to relieve him: I not doubt
  He came alive to land.
ALONSO
  No, no, he's gone.
SEBASTIAN
  Sir, you may thank yourself for this great loss,
  That would not bless our Europe with your daughter,

But rather lose her to an African;
Where she at least is banish'd from your eye,
Who hath cause to wet the grief on't.

ALONSO
Prithee, peace.

SEBASTIAN
You were kneel'd to and importuned otherwise
By all of us, and the fair soul herself
Weigh'd between loathness and obedience, at
Which end o' the beam should bow. We have lost your
son,
I fear, for ever: Milan and Naples have
More widows in them of this business' making
Than we bring men to comfort them:
The fault's your own.

ALONSO
So is the dear'st o' the loss.

GONZALO
My lord Sebastian,
The truth you speak doth lack some gentleness
And time to speak it in: you rub the sore,
When you should bring the plaster.

SEBASTIAN
Very well.

ANTONIO
And most chirurgeonly.

GONZALO
It is foul weather in us all, good sir,
When you are cloudy.

SEBASTIAN
Foul weather?

ANTONIO
Very foul.

GONZALO

Had I plantation of this isle, my lord,--
ANTONIO
He'ld sow't with nettle-seed.
SEBASTIAN
Or docks, or mallows.
GONZALO
And were the king on't, what would I do?
SEBASTIAN
'Scape being drunk for want of wine.
GONZALO
I' the commonwealth I would by contraries
Execute all things; for no kind of traffic
Would I admit; no name of magistrate;
Letters should not be known; riches, poverty,
And use of service, none; contract, succession,
Bourn, bound of land, tilth, vineyard, none;
No use of metal, corn, or wine, or oil;
No occupation; all men idle, all;
And women too, but innocent and pure;
No sovereignty;--
SEBASTIAN
Yet he would be king on't.
ANTONIO
The latter end of his commonwealth forgets the
beginning.
GONZALO
All things in common nature should produce
Without sweat or endeavour: treason, felony,
Sword, pike, knife, gun, or need of any engine,
Would I not have; but nature should bring forth,
Of its own kind, all foison, all abundance,
To feed my innocent people.
SEBASTIAN
No marrying 'mong his subjects?

ANTONIO
  None, man; all idle: whores and knaves.
GONZALO
  I would with such perfection govern, sir,
  To excel the golden age.
SEBASTIAN
  God save his majesty!
ANTONIO
  Long live Gonzalo!
GONZALO
  And,--do you mark me, sir?
ALONSO
  Prithee, no more: thou dost talk nothing to me.
GONZALO
  I do well believe your highness; and
  did it to minister occasion to these gentlemen,
  who are of such sensible and nimble lungs that
  they always use to laugh at nothing.
ANTONIO
  'Twas you we laughed at.
GONZALO
  Who in this kind of merry fooling am nothing
  to you: so you may continue and laugh at
  nothing still.
ANTONIO
  What a blow was there given!
SEBASTIAN
  An it had not fallen flat-long.
GONZALO
  You are gentlemen of brave metal; you would lift
  the moon out of her sphere, if she would continue
  in it five weeks without changing.

  Enter ARIEL, invisible, playing solemn music

SEBASTIAN

We would so, and then go a bat-fowling.

ANTONIO

Nay, good my lord, be not angry.

GONZALO

No, I warrant you; I will not adventure
my discretion so weakly. Will you laugh
me asleep, for I am very heavy?

ANTONIO

Go sleep, and hear us.

All sleep except ALONSO, SEBASTIAN, and ANTONIO

ALONSO

What, all so soon asleep! I wish mine eyes
Would, with themselves, shut up my thoughts: I find
They are inclined to do so.

SEBASTIAN

Please you, sir,
Do not omit the heavy offer of it:
It seldom visits sorrow; when it doth,
It is a comforter.

ANTONIO

We two, my lord,
Will guard your person while you take your rest,
And watch your safety.

ALONSO

Thank you. Wondrous heavy.

ALONSO sleeps. Exit ARIEL

SEBASTIAN

What a strange drowsiness possesses them!

ANTONIO

It is the quality o' the climate.

SEBASTIAN
   Why
   Doth it not then our eyelids sink? I find not
   Myself disposed to sleep.
ANTONIO
   Nor I; my spirits are nimble.
   They fell together all, as by consent;
   They dropp'd, as by a thunder-stroke. What might,
   Worthy Sebastian? O, what might?--No more:--
   And yet me thinks I see it in thy face,
   What thou shouldst be: the occasion speaks thee, and
   My strong imagination sees a crown
   Dropping upon thy head.
SEBASTIAN
   What, art thou waking?
ANTONIO
   Do you not hear me speak?
SEBASTIAN
   I do; and surely
   It is a sleepy language and thou speak'st
   Out of thy sleep. What is it thou didst say?
   This is a strange repose, to be asleep
   With eyes wide open; standing, speaking, moving,
   And yet so fast asleep.
ANTONIO
   Noble Sebastian,
   Thou let'st thy fortune sleep--die, rather; wink'st
   Whiles thou art waking.
SEBASTIAN
   Thou dost snore distinctly;
   There's meaning in thy snores.
ANTONIO
   I am more serious than my custom: you
   Must be so too, if heed me; which to do

Trebles thee o'er.
SEBASTIAN
 Well, I am standing water.
ANTONIO
 I'll teach you how to flow.
SEBASTIAN
 Do so: to ebb
 Hereditary sloth instructs me.
ANTONIO
 O,
 If you but knew how you the purpose cherish
 Whiles thus you mock it! how, in stripping it,
 You more invest it! Ebbing men, indeed,
 Most often do so near the bottom run
 By their own fear or sloth.
SEBASTIAN
 Prithee, say on:
 The setting of thine eye and cheek proclaim
 A matter from thee, and a birth indeed
 Which throes thee much to yield.
ANTONIO
 Thus, sir:
 Although this lord of weak remembrance, this,
 Who shall be of as little memory
 When he is earth'd, hath here almost persuade,--
 For he's a spirit of persuasion, only
 Professes to persuade,--the king his son's alive,
 'Tis as impossible that he's undrown'd
 And he that sleeps here swims.
SEBASTIAN
 I have no hope
 That he's undrown'd.
ANTONIO
 O, out of that 'no hope'

What great hope have you! no hope that way is
Another way so high a hope that even
Ambition cannot pierce a wink beyond,
But doubt discovery there. Will you grant with me
That Ferdinand is drown'd?
SEBASTIAN
He's gone.
ANTONIO
Then, tell me,
Who's the next heir of Naples?
SEBASTIAN
Claribel.
ANTONIO
She that is queen of Tunis; she that dwells
Ten leagues beyond man's life; she that from Naples
Can have no note, unless the sun were post--
The man i' the moon's too slow--till new-born chins
Be rough and razorable; she that--from whom?
We all were sea-swallow'd, though some cast again,
And by that destiny to perform an act
Whereof what's past is prologue, what to come
In yours and my discharge.
SEBASTIAN
What stuff is this! how say you?
'Tis true, my brother's daughter's queen of Tunis;
So is she heir of Naples; 'twixt which regions
There is some space.
ANTONIO
A space whose every cubit
Seems to cry out, 'How shall that Claribel
Measure us back to Naples? Keep in Tunis,
And let Sebastian wake.' Say, this were death
That now hath seized them; why, they were no worse
Than now they are. There be that can rule Naples

As well as he that sleeps; lords that can prate
As amply and unnecessarily
As this Gonzalo; I myself could make
A chough of as deep chat. O, that you bore
The mind that I do! what a sleep were this
For your advancement! Do you understand me?
SEBASTIAN
Methinks I do.
ANTONIO
And how does your content
Tender your own good fortune?
SEBASTIAN
I remember
You did supplant your brother Prospero.
ANTONIO
True:
And look how well my garments sit upon me;
Much feater than before: my brother's servants
Were then my fellows; now they are my men.
SEBASTIAN
But, for your conscience?
ANTONIO
Ay, sir; where lies that? if 'twere a kibe,
'Twould put me to my slipper: but I feel not
This deity in my bosom: twenty consciences,
That stand 'twixt me and Milan, candied be they
And melt ere they molest! Here lies your brother,
No better than the earth he lies upon,
If he were that which now he's like, that's dead;
Whom I, with this obedient steel, three inches of it,
Can lay to bed for ever; whiles you, doing thus,
To the perpetual wink for aye might put
This ancient morsel, this Sir Prudence, who
Should not upbraid our course. For all the rest,

They'll take suggestion as a cat laps milk;
They'll tell the clock to any business that
We say befits the hour.
SEBASTIAN
Thy case, dear friend,
Shall be my precedent; as thou got'st Milan,
I'll come by Naples. Draw thy sword: one stroke
Shall free thee from the tribute which thou payest;
And I the king shall love thee.
ANTONIO
Draw together;
And when I rear my hand, do you the like,
To fall it on Gonzalo.
SEBASTIAN
O, but one word.

They talk apart

Re-enter ARIEL, invisible

ARIEL
My master through his art foresees the danger
That you, his friend, are in; and sends me forth--
For else his project dies--to keep them living.

Sings in GONZALO's ear

While you here do snoring lie,
Open-eyed conspiracy
His time doth take.
If of life you keep a care,
Shake off slumber, and beware:
Awake, awake!
ANTONIO
Then let us both be sudden.

GONZALO
Now, good angels
Preserve the king.

They wake

ALONSO
Why, how now? ho, awake! Why are you drawn?
Wherefore this ghastly looking?
GONZALO
What's the matter?
SEBASTIAN
Whiles we stood here securing your repose,
Even now, we heard a hollow burst of bellowing
Like bulls, or rather lions: did't not wake you?
It struck mine ear most terribly.
ALONSO
I heard nothing.
ANTONIO
O, 'twas a din to fright a monster's ear,
To make an earthquake! sure, it was the roar
Of a whole herd of lions.
ALONSO
Heard you this, Gonzalo?
GONZALO
Upon mine honour, sir, I heard a humming,
And that a strange one too, which did awake me:
I shaked you, sir, and cried: as mine eyes open'd,
I saw their weapons drawn: there was a noise,
That's verily. 'Tis best we stand upon our guard,
Or that we quit this place; let's draw our weapons.
ALONSO
Lead off this ground; and let's make further search
For my poor son.
GONZALO

Heavens keep him from these beasts!
For he is, sure, i' the island.

ALONSO
Lead away.

ARIEL
Prospero my lord shall know what I have done:
So, king, go safely on to seek thy son.

Exeunt

SCENE II.

Another part of the island.

Enter CALIBAN with a burden of wood. A noise of thunder heard

CALIBAN
All the infections that the sun sucks up
From bogs, fens, flats, on Prosper fall and make him
By inch-meal a disease! His spirits hear me
And yet I needs must curse. But they'll nor pinch,
Fright me with urchin--shows, pitch me i' the mire,
Nor lead me, like a firebrand, in the dark
Out of my way, unless he bid 'em; but
For every trifle are they set upon me;
Sometime like apes that mow and chatter at me
And after bite me, then like hedgehogs which
Lie tumbling in my barefoot way and mount
Their pricks at my footfall; sometime am I
All wound with adders who with cloven tongues
Do hiss me into madness.

Enter TRINCULO

Lo, now, lo!
Here comes a spirit of his, and to torment me

49

For bringing wood in slowly. I'll fall flat;
Perchance he will not mind me.
TRINCULO
Here's neither bush nor shrub, to bear off
any weather at all, and another storm brewing;
I hear it sing i' the wind: yond same black
cloud, yond huge one, looks like a foul
bombard that would shed his liquor. If it
should thunder as it did before, I know not
where to hide my head: yond same cloud cannot
choose but fall by pailfuls. What have we
here? a man or a fish? dead or alive? A fish:
he smells like a fish; a very ancient and fish-
like smell; a kind of not of the newest Poor-
John. A strange fish! Were I in England now,
as once I was, and had but this fish painted,
not a holiday fool there but would give a piece
of silver: there would this monster make a
man; any strange beast there makes a man:
when they will not give a doit to relieve a lame
beggar, they will lazy out ten to see a dead
Indian. Legged like a man and his fins like
arms! Warm o' my troth! I do now let loose
my opinion; hold it no longer: this is no fish,
but an islander, that hath lately suffered by a
thunderbolt.

Thunder

Alas, the storm is come again! my best way is to
creep under his gaberdine; there is no other
shelter hereabouts: misery acquaints a man with
strange bed-fellows. I will here shroud till the
dregs of the storm be past.

Enter STEPHANO, singing: a bottle in his hand

STEPHANO
   I shall no more to sea, to sea,
   Here shall I die ashore--
   This is a very scurvy tune to sing at a man's
   funeral: well, here's my comfort.

Drinks

Sings

   The master, the swabber, the boatswain and I,
   The gunner and his mate
   Loved Mall, Meg and Marian and Margery,
   But none of us cared for Kate;
   For she had a tongue with a tang,
   Would cry to a sailor, Go hang!
   She loved not the savour of tar nor of pitch,
   Yet a tailor might scratch her where'er she did itch:
   Then to sea, boys, and let her go hang!
   This is a scurvy tune too: but here's my comfort.

Drinks

CALIBAN
   Do not torment me: Oh!
STEPHANO
   What's the matter? Have we devils here? Do you put
   tricks upon's with savages and men of Ind, ha? I
   have not scaped drowning to be afeard now of your
   four legs; for it hath been said, As proper a man as
   ever went on four legs cannot make him give ground;
   and it shall be said so again while Stephano
   breathes at's nostrils.
CALIBAN

The spirit torments me; Oh!
STEPHANO

This is some monster of the isle with four legs, who
hath got, as I take it, an ague. Where the devil
should he learn our language? I will give him some
relief, if it be but for that. if I can recover him
and keep him tame and get to Naples with him, he's a
present for any emperor that ever trod on neat's leather.
CALIBAN

Do not torment me, prithee; I'll bring my wood home
faster.
STEPHANO

He's in his fit now and does not talk after the
wisest. He shall taste of my bottle: if he have
never drunk wine afore will go near to remove his
fit. If I can recover him and keep him tame, I will
not take too much for him; he shall pay for him that
hath him, and that soundly.
CALIBAN

Thou dost me yet but little hurt; thou wilt anon, I
know it by thy trembling: now Prosper works upon thee.
STEPHANO

Come on your ways; open your mouth; here is that
which will give language to you, cat: open your
mouth; this will shake your shaking, I can tell you,
and that soundly: you cannot tell who's your friend:
open your chaps again.
TRINCULO

I should know that voice: it should be--but he is
drowned; and these are devils: O defend me!
STEPHANO

Four legs and two voices: a most delicate monster!
His forward voice now is to speak well of his
friend; his backward voice is to utter foul speeches

and to detract. If all the wine in my bottle will
recover him, I will help his ague. Come. Amen! I
will pour some in thy other mouth.

TRINCULO

Stephano!

STEPHANO

Doth thy other mouth call me? Mercy, mercy! This is
a devil, and no monster: I will leave him; I have no
long spoon.

TRINCULO

Stephano! If thou beest Stephano, touch me and
speak to me: for I am Trinculo--be not afeard--thy
good friend Trinculo.

STEPHANO

If thou beest Trinculo, come forth: I'll pull thee
by the lesser legs: if any be Trinculo's legs,
these are they. Thou art very Trinculo indeed! How
camest thou to be the siege of this moon-calf? can
he vent Trinculos?

TRINCULO

I took him to be killed with a thunder-stroke. But
art thou not drowned, Stephano? I hope now thou art
not drowned. Is the storm overblown? I hid me
under the dead moon-calf's gaberdine for fear of
the storm. And art thou living, Stephano? O
Stephano, two Neapolitans 'scaped!

STEPHANO

Prithee, do not turn me about; my stomach is not
constant.

CALIBAN

[Aside] These be fine things, an if they be
not sprites.
That's a brave god and bears celestial liquor.
I will kneel to him.

STEPHANO

How didst thou 'scape? How camest thou hither?
swear by this bottle how thou camest hither. I
escaped upon a butt of sack which the sailors
heaved o'erboard, by this bottle; which I made of
the bark of a tree with mine own hands since I was
cast ashore.

CALIBAN

I'll swear upon that bottle to be thy true subject;
for the liquor is not earthly.

STEPHANO

Here; swear then how thou escapedst.

TRINCULO

Swum ashore. man, like a duck: I can swim like a
duck, I'll be sworn.

STEPHANO

Here, kiss the book. Though thou canst swim like a
duck, thou art made like a goose.

TRINCULO

O Stephano. hast any more of this?

STEPHANO

The whole butt, man: my cellar is in a rock by the
sea-side where my wine is hid. How now, moon-calf!
how does thine ague?

CALIBAN

Hast thou not dropp'd from heaven?

STEPHANO

Out o' the moon, I do assure thee: I was the man i'
the moon when time was.

CALIBAN

I have seen thee in her and I do adore thee:
My mistress show'd me thee and thy dog and thy bush.

STEPHANO

Come, swear to that; kiss the book: I will furnish

it anon with new contents swear.

TRINCULO

By this good light, this is a very shallow monster!
I afeard of him! A very weak monster! The man i'
the moon! A most poor credulous monster! Well
drawn, monster, in good sooth!

CALIBAN

I'll show thee every fertile inch o' th' island;
And I will kiss thy foot: I prithee, be my god.

TRINCULO

By this light, a most perfidious and drunken
monster! when 's god's asleep, he'll rob his bottle.

CALIBAN

I'll kiss thy foot; I'll swear myself thy subject.

STEPHANO

Come on then; down, and swear.

TRINCULO

I shall laugh myself to death at this puppy-headed
monster. A most scurvy monster! I could find in my
heart to beat him,--

STEPHANO

Come, kiss.

TRINCULO

But that the poor monster's in drink: an abominable
monster!

CALIBAN

I'll show thee the best springs; I'll pluck thee berries;
I'll fish for thee and get thee wood enough.
A plague upon the tyrant that I serve!
I'll bear him no more sticks, but follow thee,
Thou wondrous man.

TRINCULO

A most ridiculous monster, to make a wonder of a
Poor drunkard!

CALIBAN
  I prithee, let me bring thee where crabs grow;
  And I with my long nails will dig thee pignuts;
  Show thee a jay's nest and instruct thee how
  To snare the nimble marmoset; I'll bring thee
  To clustering filberts and sometimes I'll get thee
  Young scamels from the rock. Wilt thou go with me?
STEPHANO
  I prithee now, lead the way without any more
  talking. Trinculo, the king and all our company
  else being drowned, we will inherit here: here;
  bear my bottle: fellow Trinculo, we'll fill him by
  and by again.
CALIBAN
  [Sings drunkenly]
  Farewell master; farewell, farewell!
TRINCULO
  A howling monster: a drunken monster!
CALIBAN
  No more dams I'll make for fish
  Nor fetch in firing
  At requiring;
  Nor scrape trencher, nor wash dish
  'Ban, 'Ban, Cacaliban
  Has a new master: get a new man.
  Freedom, hey-day! hey-day, freedom! freedom,
  hey-day, freedom!
STEPHANO
  O brave monster! Lead the way.

                                        Exeunt

ACT III

SCENE I.

Before PROSPERO'S Cell.

Enter FERDINAND, bearing a log

FERDINAND
    There be some sports are painful, and their labour
    Delight in them sets off: some kinds of baseness
    Are nobly undergone and most poor matters
    Point to rich ends. This my mean task
    Would be as heavy to me as odious, but
    The mistress which I serve quickens what's dead
    And makes my labours pleasures: O, she is
    Ten times more gentle than her father's crabbed,
    And he's composed of harshness. I must remove
    Some thousands of these logs and pile them up,
    Upon a sore injunction: my sweet mistress
    Weeps when she sees me work, and says, such baseness
    Had never like executor. I forget:
    But these sweet thoughts do even refresh my labours,
    Most busy lest, when I do it.

    Enter MIRANDA; and PROSPERO at a distance, unseen

MIRANDA
    Alas, now, pray you,
    Work not so hard: I would the lightning had
    Burnt up those logs that you are enjoin'd to pile!
    Pray, set it down and rest you: when this burns,
    'Twill weep for having wearied you. My father
    Is hard at study; pray now, rest yourself;
    He's safe for these three hours.

FERDINAND
    O most dear mistress,
    The sun will set before I shall discharge
    What I must strive to do.
MIRANDA
    If you'll sit down,
    I'll bear your logs the while: pray, give me that;
    I'll carry it to the pile.
FERDINAND
    No, precious creature;
    I had rather crack my sinews, break my back,
    Than you should such dishonour undergo,
    While I sit lazy by.
MIRANDA
    It would become me
    As well as it does you: and I should do it
    With much more ease; for my good will is to it,
    And yours it is against.
PROSPERO
    Poor worm, thou art infected!
    This visitation shows it.
MIRANDA
    You look wearily.
FERDINAND
    No, noble mistress;'tis fresh morning with me
    When you are by at night. I do beseech you--
    Chiefly that I might set it in my prayers--
    What is your name?
MIRANDA
    Miranda.--O my father,
    I have broke your hest to say so!
FERDINAND
    Admired Miranda!
    Indeed the top of admiration! worth

What's dearest to the world! Full many a lady
I have eyed with best regard and many a time
The harmony of their tongues hath into bondage
Brought my too diligent ear: for several virtues
Have I liked several women; never any
With so fun soul, but some defect in her
Did quarrel with the noblest grace she owed
And put it to the foil: but you, O you,
So perfect and so peerless, are created
Of every creature's best!

MIRANDA

I do not know
One of my sex; no woman's face remember,
Save, from my glass, mine own; nor have I seen
More that I may call men than you, good friend,
And my dear father: how features are abroad,
I am skilless of; but, by my modesty,
The jewel in my dower, I would not wish
Any companion in the world but you,
Nor can imagination form a shape,
Besides yourself, to like of. But I prattle
Something too wildly and my father's precepts
I therein do forget.

FERDINAND

I am in my condition
A prince, Miranda; I do think, a king;
I would, not so!--and would no more endure
This wooden slavery than to suffer
The flesh-fly blow my mouth. Hear my soul speak:
The very instant that I saw you, did
My heart fly to your service; there resides,
To make me slave to it; and for your sake
Am I this patient log--man.

MIRANDA

Do you love me?
FERDINAND
O heaven, O earth, bear witness to this sound
And crown what I profess with kind event
If I speak true! if hollowly, invert
What best is boded me to mischief! I
Beyond all limit of what else i' the world
Do love, prize, honour you.
MIRANDA
I am a fool
To weep at what I am glad of.
PROSPERO
Fair encounter
Of two most rare affections! Heavens rain grace
On that which breeds between 'em!
FERDINAND
Wherefore weep you?
MIRANDA
At mine unworthiness that dare not offer
What I desire to give, and much less take
What I shall die to want. But this is trifling;
And all the more it seeks to hide itself,
The bigger bulk it shows. Hence, bashful cunning!
And prompt me, plain and holy innocence!
I am your wife, if you will marry me;
If not, I'll die your maid: to be your fellow
You may deny me; but I'll be your servant,
Whether you will or no.
FERDINAND
My mistress, dearest;
And I thus humble ever.
MIRANDA
My husband, then?
FERDINAND

Ay, with a heart as willing
As bondage e'er of freedom: here's my hand.

MIRANDA
And mine, with my heart in't; and now farewell
Till half an hour hence.

FERDINAND
A thousand thousand!

Exeunt FERDINAND and MIRANDA severally

PROSPERO
So glad of this as they I cannot be,
Who are surprised withal; but my rejoicing
At nothing can be more. I'll to my book,
For yet ere supper-time must I perform
Much business appertaining.

Exit

SCENE II.

Another part of the island.

Enter CALIBAN, STEPHANO, and TRINCULO

STEPHANO
Tell not me; when the butt is out, we will drink
water; not a drop before: therefore bear up, and
board 'em. Servant-monster, drink to me.

TRINCULO
Servant-monster! the folly of this island! They
say there's but five upon this isle: we are three
of them; if th' other two be brained like us, the
state totters.

STEPHANO
Drink, servant-monster, when I bid thee: thy eyes

are almost set in thy head.

TRINCULO

Where should they be set else? he were a brave
monster indeed, if they were set in his tail.

STEPHANO

My man-monster hath drown'd his tongue in sack:
for my part, the sea cannot drown me; I swam, ere I
could recover the shore, five and thirty leagues off
and on. By this light, thou shalt be my lieutenant,
monster, or my standard.

TRINCULO

Your lieutenant, if you list; he's no standard.

STEPHANO

We'll not run, Monsieur Monster.

TRINCULO

Nor go neither; but you'll lie like dogs and yet say
nothing neither.

STEPHANO

Moon-calf, speak once in thy life, if thou beest a
good moon-calf.

CALIBAN

How does thy honour? Let me lick thy shoe.
I'll not serve him; he's not valiant.

TRINCULO

Thou liest, most ignorant monster: I am in case to
justle a constable. Why, thou deboshed fish thou,
was there ever man a coward that hath drunk so much
sack as I to-day? Wilt thou tell a monstrous lie,
being but half a fish and half a monster?

CALIBAN

Lo, how he mocks me! wilt thou let him, my lord?

TRINCULO

'Lord' quoth he! That a monster should be such a
natural!

CALIBAN

Lo, lo, again! bite him to death, I prithee.

STEPHANO

Trinculo, keep a good tongue in your head: if you
prove a mutineer,--the next tree! The poor monster's
my subject and he shall not suffer indignity.

CALIBAN

I thank my noble lord. Wilt thou be pleased to
hearken once again to the suit I made to thee?

STEPHANO

Marry, will I kneel and repeat it; I will stand,
and so shall Trinculo.

Enter ARIEL, invisible

CALIBAN

As I told thee before, I am subject to a tyrant, a
sorcerer, that by his cunning hath cheated me of the
island.

ARIEL

Thou liest.

CALIBAN

Thou liest, thou jesting monkey, thou: I would my
valiant master would destroy thee! I do not lie.

STEPHANO

Trinculo, if you trouble him any more in's tale, by
this hand, I will supplant some of your teeth.

TRINCULO

Why, I said nothing.

STEPHANO

Mum, then, and no more. Proceed.

CALIBAN

I say, by sorcery he got this isle;
From me he got it. if thy greatness will
Revenge it on him,--for I know thou darest,

But this thing dare not,--
STEPHANO
That's most certain.
CALIBAN
Thou shalt be lord of it and I'll serve thee.
STEPHANO
How now shall this be compassed?
Canst thou bring me to the party?
CALIBAN
Yea, yea, my lord: I'll yield him thee asleep,
Where thou mayst knock a nail into his bead.
ARIEL
Thou liest; thou canst not.
CALIBAN
What a pied ninny's this! Thou scurvy patch!
I do beseech thy greatness, give him blows
And take his bottle from him: when that's gone
He shall drink nought but brine; for I'll not show him
Where the quick freshes are.
STEPHANO
Trinculo, run into no further danger:
interrupt the monster one word further, and,
by this hand, I'll turn my mercy out o' doors
and make a stock-fish of thee.
TRINCULO
Why, what did I? I did nothing. I'll go farther
off.
STEPHANO
Didst thou not say he lied?
ARIEL
Thou liest.
STEPHANO
Do I so? take thou that.

Beats TRINCULO

As you like this, give me the lie another time.
TRINCULO
I did not give the lie. Out o' your
wits and bearing too? A pox o' your bottle!
this can sack and drinking do. A murrain on
your monster, and the devil take your fingers!
CALIBAN
Ha, ha, ha!
STEPHANO
Now, forward with your tale. Prithee, stand farther
off.
CALIBAN
Beat him enough: after a little time
I'll beat him too.
STEPHANO
Stand farther. Come, proceed.
CALIBAN
Why, as I told thee, 'tis a custom with him,
I' th' afternoon to sleep: there thou mayst brain him,
Having first seized his books, or with a log
Batter his skull, or paunch him with a stake,
Or cut his wezand with thy knife. Remember
First to possess his books; for without them
He's but a sot, as I am, nor hath not
One spirit to command: they all do hate him
As rootedly as I. Burn but his books.
He has brave utensils,--for so he calls them--
Which when he has a house, he'll deck withal
And that most deeply to consider is
The beauty of his daughter; he himself
Calls her a nonpareil: I never saw a woman,
But only Sycorax my dam and she;
But she as far surpasseth Sycorax

As great'st does least.

STEPHANO

Is it so brave a lass?

CALIBAN

Ay, lord; she will become thy bed, I warrant.
And bring thee forth brave brood.

STEPHANO

Monster, I will kill this man: his daughter and I
will be king and queen--save our graces!--and
Trinculo and thyself shall be viceroys. Dost thou
like the plot, Trinculo?

TRINCULO

Excellent.

STEPHANO

Give me thy hand: I am sorry I beat thee; but,
while thou livest, keep a good tongue in thy head.

CALIBAN

Within this half hour will he be asleep:
Wilt thou destroy him then?

STEPHANO

Ay, on mine honour.

ARIEL

This will I tell my master.

CALIBAN

Thou makest me merry; I am full of pleasure:
Let us be jocund: will you troll the catch
You taught me but while-ere?

STEPHANO

At thy request, monster, I will do reason, any
reason. Come on, Trinculo, let us sing.

Sings

Flout 'em and scout 'em
And scout 'em and flout 'em

Thought is free.
CALIBAN
That's not the tune.

Ariel plays the tune on a tabour and pipe

STEPHANO
What is this same?
TRINCULO
This is the tune of our catch, played by the picture
of Nobody.
STEPHANO
If thou beest a man, show thyself in thy likeness:
if thou beest a devil, take't as thou list.
TRINCULO
O, forgive me my sins!
STEPHANO
He that dies pays all debts: I defy thee. Mercy upon us!
CALIBAN
Art thou afeard?
STEPHANO
No, monster, not I.
CALIBAN
Be not afeard; the isle is full of noises,
Sounds and sweet airs, that give delight and hurt not.
Sometimes a thousand twangling instruments
Will hum about mine ears, and sometime voices
That, if I then had waked after long sleep,
Will make me sleep again: and then, in dreaming,
The clouds methought would open and show riches
Ready to drop upon me that, when I waked,
I cried to dream again.
STEPHANO
This will prove a brave kingdom to me, where I shall
have my music for nothing.

CALIBAN
  When Prospero is destroyed.
STEPHANO
  That shall be by and by: I remember the story.
TRINCULO
  The sound is going away; let's follow it, and
  after do our work.
STEPHANO
  Lead, monster; we'll follow. I would I could see
  this tabourer; he lays it on.
TRINCULO
  Wilt come? I'll follow, Stephano.

Exeunt

SCENE III.

Another part of the island.

*Enter ALONSO, SEBASTIAN, ANTONIO, GONZALO,
ADRIAN, FRANCISCO, and others*

GONZALO
  By'r lakin, I can go no further, sir;
  My old bones ache: here's a maze trod indeed
  Through forth-rights and meanders! By your patience,
  I needs must rest me.
ALONSO
  Old lord, I cannot blame thee,
  Who am myself attach'd with weariness,
  To the dulling of my spirits: sit down, and rest.
  Even here I will put off my hope and keep it
  No longer for my flatterer: he is drown'd
  Whom thus we stray to find, and the sea mocks
  Our frustrate search on land. Well, let him go.
ANTONIO

[Aside to SEBASTIAN] I am right glad that he's so
    out of hope.
    Do not, for one repulse, forego the purpose
    That you resolved to effect.
SEBASTIAN
[Aside to ANTONIO] The next advantage
    Will we take throughly.
ANTONIO
[Aside to SEBASTIAN] Let it be to-night;
    For, now they are oppress'd with travel, they
    Will not, nor cannot, use such vigilance
    As when they are fresh.
SEBASTIAN
[Aside to ANTONIO] I say, to-night: no more.

Solemn and strange music

ALONSO
    What harmony is this? My good friends, hark!
GONZALO
    Marvellous sweet music!

Enter PROSPERO above, invisible. Enter several strange
Shapes, bringing in a banquet; they dance about it with
gentle actions of salutation; and, inviting the King, & c. to
eat, they depart

ALONSO
    Give us kind keepers, heavens! What were these?
SEBASTIAN
    A living drollery. Now I will believe
    That there are unicorns, that in Arabia
    There is one tree, the phoenix' throne, one phoenix
    At this hour reigning there.
ANTONIO
    I'll believe both;

And what does else want credit, come to me,
And I'll be sworn 'tis true: travellers ne'er did
lie,
Though fools at home condemn 'em.
GONZALO
If in Naples
I should report this now, would they believe me?
If I should say, I saw such islanders--
For, certes, these are people of the island--
Who, though they are of monstrous shape, yet, note,
Their manners are more gentle-kind than of
Our human generation you shall find
Many, nay, almost any.
PROSPERO
[Aside] Honest lord,
Thou hast said well; for some of you there present
Are worse than devils.
ALONSO
I cannot too much muse
Such shapes, such gesture and such sound, expressing,
Although they want the use of tongue, a kind
Of excellent dumb discourse.
PROSPERO
[Aside]   Praise in departing.
FRANCISCO
They vanish'd strangely.
SEBASTIAN
No matter, since
They have left their viands behind; for we have
stomachs.
Will't please you taste of what is here?
ALONSO
Not I.
GONZALO

Faith, sir, you need not fear. When we were boys,
Who would believe that there were mountaineers
Dew-lapp'd like bulls, whose throats had hanging at 'em
Wallets of flesh? or that there were such men
Whose heads stood in their breasts? which now we find
Each putter-out of five for one will bring us
Good warrant of.
ALONSO
I will stand to and feed,
Although my last: no matter, since I feel
The best is past. Brother, my lord the duke,
Stand to and do as we.

Thunder and lightning. Enter ARIEL, like a harpy; claps his
wings upon the table; and, with a quaint device, the banquet
vanishes

ARIEL
You are three men of sin, whom Destiny,
That hath to instrument this lower world
And what is in't, the never-surfeited sea
Hath caused to belch up you; and on this island
Where man doth not inhabit; you 'mongst men
Being most unfit to live. I have made you mad;
And even with such-like valour men hang and drown
Their proper selves.

ALONSO, SEBASTIAN & c. draw their swords

You fools! I and my fellows
Are ministers of Fate: the elements,
Of whom your swords are temper'd, may as well
Wound the loud winds, or with bemock'd-at stabs
Kill the still-closing waters, as diminish
One dowle that's in my plume: my fellow-ministers

71

Are like invulnerable. If you could hurt,
Your swords are now too massy for your strengths
And will not be uplifted. But remember--
For that's my business to you--that you three
From Milan did supplant good Prospero;
Exposed unto the sea, which hath requit it,
Him and his innocent child: for which foul deed
The powers, delaying, not forgetting, have
Incensed the seas and shores, yea, all the creatures,
Against your peace. Thee of thy son, Alonso,
They have bereft; and do pronounce by me:
Lingering perdition, worse than any death
Can be at once, shall step by step attend
You and your ways; whose wraths to guard you from--
Which here, in this most desolate isle, else falls
Upon your heads--is nothing but heart-sorrow
And a clear life ensuing.

*He vanishes in thunder; then, to soft music enter the Shapes
again, and dance, with mocks and mows, and carrying out
the table*

PROSPERO
Bravely the figure of this harpy hast thou
Perform'd, my Ariel; a grace it had, devouring:
Of my instruction hast thou nothing bated
In what thou hadst to say: so, with good life
And observation strange, my meaner ministers
Their several kinds have done. My high charms work
And these mine enemies are all knit up
In their distractions; they now are in my power;
And in these fits I leave them, while I visit
Young Ferdinand, whom they suppose is drown'd,
And his and mine loved darling.

72

Exit above

GONZALO
I' the name of something holy, sir, why stand you
In this strange stare?
ALONSO
O, it is monstrous, monstrous:
Methought the billows spoke and told me of it;
The winds did sing it to me, and the thunder,
That deep and dreadful organ-pipe, pronounced
The name of Prosper: it did bass my trespass.
Therefore my son i' the ooze is bedded, and
I'll seek him deeper than e'er plummet sounded
And with him there lie mudded.

Exit

SEBASTIAN
But one fiend at a time,
I'll fight their legions o'er.
ANTONIO
I'll be thy second.

Exeunt SEBASTIAN, and ANTONIO

GONZALO
All three of them are desperate: their great guilt,
Like poison given to work a great time after,
Now 'gins to bite the spirits. I do beseech you
That are of suppler joints, follow them swiftly
And hinder them from what this ecstasy
May now provoke them to.
ADRIAN
Follow, I pray you.

Exeunt

ACT IV

SCENE I.

Before PROSPERO'S cell.

Enter PROSPERO, FERDINAND, and MIRANDA

PROSPERO

    If I have too austerely punish'd you,
    Your compensation makes amends, for I
    Have given you here a third of mine own life,
    Or that for which I live; who once again
    I tender to thy hand: all thy vexations
    Were but my trials of thy love and thou
    Hast strangely stood the test here, afore Heaven,
    I ratify this my rich gift. O Ferdinand,
    Do not smile at me that I boast her off,
    For thou shalt find she will outstrip all praise
    And make it halt behind her.

FERDINAND

    I do believe it
    Against an oracle.

PROSPERO

    Then, as my gift and thine own acquisition
    Worthily purchased take my daughter: but
    If thou dost break her virgin-knot before
    All sanctimonious ceremonies may
    With full and holy rite be minister'd,
    No sweet aspersion shall the heavens let fall
    To make this contract grow: but barren hate,
    Sour-eyed disdain and discord shall bestrew
    The union of your bed with weeds so loathly
    That you shall hate it both: therefore take heed,
    As Hymen's lamps shall light you.

FERDINAND
    As I hope
    For quiet days, fair issue and long life,
    With such love as 'tis now, the murkiest den,
    The most opportune place, the strong'st suggestion.
    Our worser genius can, shall never melt
    Mine honour into lust, to take away
    The edge of that day's celebration
    When I shall think: or Phoebus' steeds are founder'd,
    Or Night kept chain'd below.
PROSPERO
    Fairly spoke.
    Sit then and talk with her; she is thine own.
    What, Ariel! my industrious servant, Ariel!

Enter ARIEL

ARIEL
    What would my potent master? here I am.
PROSPERO
    Thou and thy meaner fellows your last service
    Did worthily perform; and I must use you
    In such another trick. Go bring the rabble,
    O'er whom I give thee power, here to this place:
    Incite them to quick motion; for I must
    Bestow upon the eyes of this young couple
    Some vanity of mine art: it is my promise,
    And they expect it from me.
ARIEL
    Presently?
PROSPERO
    Ay, with a twink.
ARIEL
    Before you can say 'come' and 'go,'
    And breathe twice and cry 'so, so,'

Each one, tripping on his toe,
Will be here with mop and mow.
Do you love me, master? no?
PROSPERO
Dearly my delicate Ariel. Do not approach
Till thou dost hear me call.
ARIEL
Well, I conceive.

Exit

PROSPERO
Look thou be true; do not give dalliance
Too much the rein: the strongest oaths are straw
To the fire i' the blood: be more abstemious,
Or else, good night your vow!
FERDINAND
I warrant you sir;
The white cold virgin snow upon my heart
Abates the ardour of my liver.
PROSPERO
Well.
Now come, my Ariel! bring a corollary,
Rather than want a spirit: appear and pertly!
No tongue! all eyes! be silent.

Soft music

Enter IRIS

IRIS
Ceres, most bounteous lady, thy rich leas
Of wheat, rye, barley, vetches, oats and pease;
Thy turfy mountains, where live nibbling sheep,
And flat meads thatch'd with stover, them to keep;

76

Thy banks with pioned and twilled brims,
Which spongy April at thy hest betrims,
To make cold nymphs chaste crowns; and thy broom
-groves,
Whose shadow the dismissed bachelor loves,
Being lass-lorn: thy pole-clipt vineyard;
And thy sea-marge, sterile and rocky-hard,
Where thou thyself dost air;--the queen o' the sky,
Whose watery arch and messenger am I,
Bids thee leave these, and with her sovereign grace,
Here on this grass-plot, in this very place,
To come and sport: her peacocks fly amain:
Approach, rich Ceres, her to entertain.

Enter CERES

CERES
Hail, many-colour'd messenger, that ne'er
Dost disobey the wife of Jupiter;
Who with thy saffron wings upon my flowers
Diffusest honey-drops, refreshing showers,
And with each end of thy blue bow dost crown
My bosky acres and my unshrubb'd down,
Rich scarf to my proud earth; why hath thy queen
Summon'd me hither, to this short-grass'd green?
IRIS
A contract of true love to celebrate;
And some donation freely to estate
On the blest lovers.
CERES
Tell me, heavenly bow,
If Venus or her son, as thou dost know,
Do now attend the queen? Since they did plot
The means that dusky Dis my daughter got,
Her and her blind boy's scandal'd company

I have forsworn.
IRIS
    Of her society
    Be not afraid: I met her deity
    Cutting the clouds towards Paphos and her son
    Dove-drawn with her. Here thought they to have done
    Some wanton charm upon this man and maid,
    Whose vows are, that no bed-right shall be paid
    Till Hymen's torch be lighted: but vain;
    Mars's hot minion is returned again;
    Her waspish-headed son has broke his arrows,
    Swears he will shoot no more but play with sparrows
    And be a boy right out.
CERES
    High'st queen of state,
    Great Juno, comes; I know her by her gait.

Enter JUNO

JUNO
    How does my bounteous sister? Go with me
    To bless this twain, that they may prosperous be
    And honour'd in their issue.

They sing:

JUNO
    Honour, riches, marriage-blessing,
    Long continuance, and increasing,
    Hourly joys be still upon you!
    Juno sings her blessings upon you.
CERES
    Earth's increase, foison plenty,
    Barns and garners never empty,
    Vines and clustering bunches growing,

Plants with goodly burthen bowing;
Spring come to you at the farthest
In the very end of harvest!
Scarcity and want shall shun you;
Ceres' blessing so is on you.

FERDINAND

This is a most majestic vision, and
Harmoniously charmingly. May I be bold
To think these spirits?

PROSPERO

Spirits, which by mine art
I have from their confines call'd to enact
My present fancies.

FERDINAND

Let me live here ever;
So rare a wonder'd father and a wife
Makes this place Paradise.

Juno and Ceres whisper, and send Iris on employment

PROSPERO

Sweet, now, silence!
Juno and Ceres whisper seriously;
There's something else to do: hush, and be mute,
Or else our spell is marr'd.

IRIS

You nymphs, call'd Naiads, of the windring brooks,
With your sedged crowns and ever-harmless looks,
Leave your crisp channels and on this green land
Answer your summons; Juno does command:
Come, temperate nymphs, and help to celebrate
A contract of true love; be not too late.

Enter certain Nymphs

You sunburnt sicklemen, of August weary,
Come hither from the furrow and be merry:
Make holiday; your rye-straw hats put on
And these fresh nymphs encounter every one
In country footing.

*Enter certain Reapers, properly habited: they join with the
Nymphs in a graceful dance; towards the end whereof
PROSPERO starts suddenly, and speaks; after which, to a
strange, hollow, and confused noise, they heavily vanish*

PROSPERO
[Aside] I had forgot that foul conspiracy
Of the beast Caliban and his confederates
Against my life: the minute of their plot
Is almost come.

To the Spirits

Well done! avoid; no more!
FERDINAND
This is strange: your father's in some passion
That works him strongly.
MIRANDA
Never till this day
Saw I him touch'd with anger so distemper'd.
PROSPERO
You do look, my son, in a moved sort,
As if you were dismay'd: be cheerful, sir.
Our revels now are ended. These our actors,
As I foretold you, were all spirits and
Are melted into air, into thin air:
And, like the baseless fabric of this vision,
The cloud-capp'd towers, the gorgeous palaces,
The solemn temples, the great globe itself,
Ye all which it inherit, shall dissolve

And, like this insubstantial pageant faded,
Leave not a rack behind. We are such stuff
As dreams are made on, and our little life
Is rounded with a sleep. Sir, I am vex'd;
Bear with my weakness; my, brain is troubled:
Be not disturb'd with my infirmity:
If you be pleased, retire into my cell
And there repose: a turn or two I'll walk,
To still my beating mind.
FERDINAND MIRANDA
We wish your peace.

Exeunt

PROSPERO
Come with a thought I thank thee, Ariel: come.

Enter ARIEL

ARIEL
Thy thoughts I cleave to. What's thy pleasure?
PROSPERO
Spirit,
We must prepare to meet with Caliban.
ARIEL
Ay, my commander: when I presented Ceres,
I thought to have told thee of it, but I fear'd
Lest I might anger thee.
PROSPERO
Say again, where didst thou leave these varlets?
ARIEL
I told you, sir, they were red-hot with drinking;
So fun of valour that they smote the air
For breathing in their faces; beat the ground
For kissing of their feet; yet always bending

81

Towards their project. Then I beat my tabour;
At which, like unback'd colts, they prick'd
    their ears,
Advanced their eyelids, lifted up their noses
As they smelt music: so I charm'd their ears
That calf-like they my lowing follow'd through
Tooth'd briers, sharp furzes, pricking goss and thorns,
Which entered their frail shins: at last I left them
I' the filthy-mantled pool beyond your cell,
There dancing up to the chins, that the foul lake
O'erstunk their feet.

PROSPERO

This was well done, my bird.
Thy shape invisible retain thou still:
The trumpery in my house, go bring it hither,
For stale to catch these thieves.

ARIEL

I go, I go.

Exit

PROSPERO

A devil, a born devil, on whose nature
Nurture can never stick; on whom my pains,
Humanely taken, all, all lost, quite lost;
And as with age his body uglier grows,
So his mind cankers. I will plague them all,
Even to roaring.

Re-enter ARIEL, loaden with glistering apparel, & c

Come, hang them on this line.

*PROSPERO and ARIEL remain invisible. Enter CALIBAN,
STEPHANO, and TRINCULO, all wet*

CALIBAN
    Pray you, tread softly, that the blind mole may not
    Hear a foot fall: we now are near his cell.
STEPHANO
    Monster, your fairy, which you say is
    a harmless fairy, has done little better than
    played the Jack with us.
TRINCULO
    Monster, I do smell all horse-piss; at
    which my nose is in great indignation.
STEPHANO
    So is mine. Do you hear, monster? If I should take
    a displeasure against you, look you,--
TRINCULO
    Thou wert but a lost monster.
CALIBAN
    Good my lord, give me thy favour still.
    Be patient, for the prize I'll bring thee to
    Shall hoodwink this mischance: therefore speak softly.
    All's hush'd as midnight yet.
TRINCULO
    Ay, but to lose our bottles in the pool,--
STEPHANO
    There is not only disgrace and dishonour in that,
    monster, but an infinite loss.
TRINCULO
    That's more to me than my wetting: yet this is your
    harmless fairy, monster.
STEPHANO
    I will fetch off my bottle, though I be o'er ears
    for my labour.
CALIBAN
    Prithee, my king, be quiet. Seest thou here,
    This is the mouth o' the cell: no noise, and enter.

Do that good mischief which may make this island
Thine own for ever, and I, thy Caliban,
For aye thy foot-licker.

STEPHANO

Give me thy hand. I do begin to have bloody thoughts.

TRINCULO

O king Stephano! O peer! O worthy Stephano! look
what a wardrobe here is for thee!

CALIBAN

Let it alone, thou fool; it is but trash.

TRINCULO

O, ho, monster! we know what belongs to a frippery.
O king Stephano!

STEPHANO

Put off that gown, Trinculo; by this hand, I'll have
that gown.

TRINCULO

Thy grace shall have it.

CALIBAN

The dropsy drown this fool I what do you mean
To dote thus on such luggage? Let's alone
And do the murder first: if he awake,
From toe to crown he'll fill our skins with pinches,
Make us strange stuff.

STEPHANO

Be you quiet, monster. Mistress line,
is not this my jerkin? Now is the jerkin under
the line: now, jerkin, you are like to lose your
hair and prove a bald jerkin.

TRINCULO

Do, do: we steal by line and level, an't like your grace.

STEPHANO

I thank thee for that jest; here's a garment for't:
wit shall not go unrewarded while I am king of this

country. 'Steal by line and level' is an excellent
pass of pate; there's another garment for't.
TRINCULO
Monster, come, put some lime upon your fingers, and
away with the rest.
CALIBAN
I will have none on't: we shall lose our time,
And all be turn'd to barnacles, or to apes
With foreheads villanous low.
STEPHANO
Monster, lay-to your fingers: help to bear this
away where my hogshead of wine is, or I'll turn you
out of my kingdom: go to, carry this.
TRINCULO
And this.
STEPHANO
Ay, and this.

*A noise of hunters heard. Enter divers Spirits, in shape of
dogs and hounds, and hunt them about, PROSPERO and
ARIEL setting them on*

PROSPERO
Hey, Mountain, hey!
ARIEL
Silver I there it goes, Silver!
PROSPERO
Fury, Fury! there, Tyrant, there! hark! hark!

CALIBAN, STEPHANO, and TRINCULO, are driven out

Go charge my goblins that they grind their joints
With dry convulsions, shorten up their sinews
With aged cramps, and more pinch-spotted make them
Than pard or cat o' mountain.

ARIEL
Hark, they roar!
PROSPERO
Let them be hunted soundly. At this hour
Lie at my mercy all mine enemies:
Shortly shall all my labours end, and thou
Shalt have the air at freedom: for a little
Follow, and do me service.

Exeunt

ACT V

SCENE I.

Before PROSPERO'S cell.

Enter PROSPERO in his magic robes, and ARIEL

PROSPERO
    Now does my project gather to a head:
    My charms crack not; my spirits obey; and time
    Goes upright with his carriage. How's the day?
ARIEL
    On the sixth hour; at which time, my lord,
    You said our work should cease.
PROSPERO
    I did say so,
    When first I raised the tempest. Say, my spirit,
    How fares the king and's followers?
ARIEL
    Confined together
    In the same fashion as you gave in charge,
    Just as you left them; all prisoners, sir,
    In the line-grove which weather-fends your cell;
    They cannot budge till your release. The king,
    His brother and yours, abide all three distracted
    And the remainder mourning over them,
    Brimful of sorrow and dismay; but chiefly
    Him that you term'd, sir, 'The good old lord Gonzalo;'
    His tears run down his beard, like winter's drops
    From eaves of reeds. Your charm so strongly works 'em
    That if you now beheld them, your affections
    Would become tender.
PROSPERO
    Dost thou think so, spirit?

ARIEL
  Mine would, sir, were I human.
PROSPERO
  And mine shall.
  Hast thou, which art but air, a touch, a feeling
  Of their afflictions, and shall not myself,
  One of their kind, that relish all as sharply,
  Passion as they, be kindlier moved than thou art?
  Though with their high wrongs I am struck to the quick,
  Yet with my nobler reason 'gaitist my fury
  Do I take part: the rarer action is
  In virtue than in vengeance: they being penitent,
  The sole drift of my purpose doth extend
  Not a frown further. Go release them, Ariel:
  My charms I'll break, their senses I'll restore,
  And they shall be themselves.
ARIEL
  I'll fetch them, sir.

Exit

PROSPERO
  Ye elves of hills, brooks, standing lakes and groves,
  And ye that on the sands with printless foot
  Do chase the ebbing Neptune and do fly him
  When he comes back; you demi-puppets that
  By moonshine do the green sour ringlets make,
  Whereof the ewe not bites, and you whose pastime
  Is to make midnight mushrooms, that rejoice
  To hear the solemn curfew; by whose aid,
  Weak masters though ye be, I have bedimm'd
  The noontide sun, call'd forth the mutinous winds,
  And 'twixt the green sea and the azured vault
  Set roaring war: to the dread rattling thunder
  Have I given fire and rifted Jove's stout oak

With his own bolt; the strong-based promontory
Have I made shake and by the spurs pluck'd up
The pine and cedar: graves at my command
Have waked their sleepers, oped, and let 'em forth
By my so potent art. But this rough magic
I here abjure, and, when I have required
Some heavenly music, which even now I do,
To work mine end upon their senses that
This airy charm is for, I'll break my staff,
Bury it certain fathoms in the earth,
And deeper than did ever plummet sound
I'll drown my book.

Solemn music

*Re-enter ARIEL before: then ALONSO, with a frantic
gesture, attended by GONZALO; SEBASTIAN and
ANTONIO in like manner, attended by ADRIAN and
FRANCISCO they all enter the circle which PROSPERO
had made, and there stand charmed; which PROSPERO
observing, speaks:*

A solemn air and the best comforter
To an unsettled fancy cure thy brains,
Now useless, boil'd within thy skull! There stand,
For you are spell-stopp'd.
Holy Gonzalo, honourable man,
Mine eyes, even sociable to the show of thine,
Fall fellowly drops. The charm dissolves apace,
And as the morning steals upon the night,
Melting the darkness, so their rising senses
Begin to chase the ignorant fumes that mantle
Their clearer reason. O good Gonzalo,
My true preserver, and a loyal sir
To him you follow'st! I will pay thy graces

Home both in word and deed. Most cruelly
Didst thou, Alonso, use me and my daughter:
Thy brother was a furtherer in the act.
Thou art pinch'd fort now, Sebastian. Flesh and blood,
You, brother mine, that entertain'd ambition,
Expell'd remorse and nature; who, with Sebastian,
Whose inward pinches therefore are most strong,
Would here have kill'd your king; I do forgive thee,
Unnatural though thou art. Their understanding
Begins to swell, and the approaching tide
Will shortly fill the reasonable shore
That now lies foul and muddy. Not one of them
That yet looks on me, or would know me Ariel,
Fetch me the hat and rapier in my cell:
I will discase me, and myself present
As I was sometime Milan: quickly, spirit;
Thou shalt ere long be free.

ARIEL sings and helps to attire him

Where the bee sucks. there suck I:
In a cowslip's bell I lie;
There I couch when owls do cry.
On the bat's back I do fly
After summer merrily.
Merrily, merrily shall I live now
Under the blossom that hangs on the bough.
PROSPERO
Why, that's my dainty Ariel! I shall miss thee:
But yet thou shalt have freedom: so, so, so.
To the king's ship, invisible as thou art:
There shalt thou find the mariners asleep
Under the hatches; the master and the boatswain
Being awake, enforce them to this place,
And presently, I prithee.

ARIEL

I drink the air before me, and return
Or ere your pulse twice beat.

Exit

GONZALO

All torment, trouble, wonder and amazement
Inhabits here: some heavenly power guide us
Out of this fearful country!

PROSPERO

Behold, sir king,
The wronged Duke of Milan, Prospero:
For more assurance that a living prince
Does now speak to thee, I embrace thy body;
And to thee and thy company I bid
A hearty welcome.

ALONSO

Whether thou best he or no,
Or some enchanted trifle to abuse me,
As late I have been, I not know: thy pulse
Beats as of flesh and blood; and, since I saw thee,
The affliction of my mind amends, with which,
I fear, a madness held me: this must crave,
An if this be at all, a most strange story.
Thy dukedom I resign and do entreat
Thou pardon me my wrongs. But how should Prospero
Be living and be here?

PROSPERO

First, noble friend,
Let me embrace thine age, whose honour cannot
Be measured or confined.

GONZALO

Whether this be
Or be not, I'll not swear.

PROSPERO
> You do yet taste
> Some subtilties o' the isle, that will not let you
> Believe things certain. Welcome, my friends all!

> *Aside to SEBASTIAN and ANTONIO*

> But you, my brace of lords, were I so minded,
> I here could pluck his highness' frown upon you
> And justify you traitors: at this time
> I will tell no tales.

SEBASTIAN
> [Aside] The devil speaks in him.

PROSPERO
> No.
> For you, most wicked sir, whom to call brother
> Would even infect my mouth, I do forgive
> Thy rankest fault; all of them; and require
> My dukedom of thee, which perforce, I know,
> Thou must restore.

ALONSO
> If thou be'st Prospero,
> Give us particulars of thy preservation;
> How thou hast met us here, who three hours since
> Were wreck'd upon this shore; where I have lost--
> How sharp the point of this remembrance is!--
> My dear son Ferdinand.

PROSPERO
> I am woe for't, sir.

ALONSO
> Irreparable is the loss, and patience
> Says it is past her cure.

PROSPERO
> I rather think
> You have not sought her help, of whose soft grace

For the like loss I have her sovereign aid
And rest myself content.
ALONSO
You the like loss!
PROSPERO
As great to me as late; and, supportable
To make the dear loss, have I means much weaker
Than you may call to comfort you, for I
Have lost my daughter.
ALONSO
A daughter?
O heavens, that they were living both in Naples,
The king and queen there! that they were, I wish
Myself were mudded in that oozy bed
Where my son lies. When did you lose your daughter?
PROSPERO
In this last tempest. I perceive these lords
At this encounter do so much admire
That they devour their reason and scarce think
Their eyes do offices of truth, their words
Are natural breath: but, howsoe'er you have
Been justled from your senses, know for certain
That I am Prospero and that very duke
Which was thrust forth of Milan, who most strangely
Upon this shore, where you were wreck'd, was landed,
To be the lord on't. No more yet of this;
For 'tis a chronicle of day by day,
Not a relation for a breakfast nor
Befitting this first meeting. Welcome, sir;
This cell's my court: here have I few attendants
And subjects none abroad: pray you, look in.
My dukedom since you have given me again,
I will requite you with as good a thing;
At least bring forth a wonder, to content ye

As much as me my dukedom.

Here PROSPERO discovers FERDINAND and MIRANDA
playing at chess

MIRANDA
Sweet lord, you play me false.
FERDINAND
No, my dear'st love,
I would not for the world.
MIRANDA
Yes, for a score of kingdoms you should wrangle,
And I would call it, fair play.
ALONSO
If this prove
A vision of the Island, one dear son
Shall I twice lose.
SEBASTIAN
A most high miracle!
FERDINAND
Though the seas threaten, they are merciful;
I have cursed them without cause.

Kneels

ALONSO
Now all the blessings
Of a glad father compass thee about!
Arise, and say how thou camest here.
MIRANDA
O, wonder!
How many goodly creatures are there here!
How beauteous mankind is! O brave new world,
That has such people in't!
PROSPERO

'Tis new to thee.
ALONSO

What is this maid with whom thou wast at play?
Your eld'st acquaintance cannot be three hours:
Is she the goddess that hath sever'd us,
And brought us thus together?
FERDINAND

Sir, she is mortal;
But by immortal Providence she's mine:
I chose her when I could not ask my father
For his advice, nor thought I had one. She
Is daughter to this famous Duke of Milan,
Of whom so often I have heard renown,
But never saw before; of whom I have
Received a second life; and second father
This lady makes him to me.
ALONSO

I am hers:
But, O, how oddly will it sound that I
Must ask my child forgiveness!
PROSPERO

There, sir, stop:
Let us not burthen our remembrance with
A heaviness that's gone.
GONZALO

I have inly wept,
Or should have spoke ere this. Look down, you god,
And on this couple drop a blessed crown!
For it is you that have chalk'd forth the way
Which brought us hither.
ALONSO

I say, Amen, Gonzalo!
GONZALO

Was Milan thrust from Milan, that his issue

Should become kings of Naples? O, rejoice
Beyond a common joy, and set it down
With gold on lasting pillars: In one voyage
Did Claribel her husband find at Tunis,
And Ferdinand, her brother, found a wife
Where he himself was lost, Prospero his dukedom
In a poor isle and all of us ourselves
When no man was his own.

ALONSO

[To FERDINAND and MIRANDA] Give me your hands:
Let grief and sorrow still embrace his heart
That doth not wish you joy!

GONZALO

Be it so! Amen!

Re-enter ARIEL, with the Master and Boatswain amazedly
following

O, look, sir, look, sir! here is more of us:
I prophesied, if a gallows were on land,
This fellow could not drown. Now, blasphemy,
That swear'st grace o'erboard, not an oath on shore?
Hast thou no mouth by land? What is the news?

Boatswain

The best news is, that we have safely found
Our king and company; the next, our ship--
Which, but three glasses since, we gave out split--
Is tight and yare and bravely rigg'd as when
We first put out to sea.

ARIEL

[Aside to PROSPERO] Sir, all this service
Have I done since I went.

PROSPERO

[Aside to ARIEL] My tricksy spirit!

ALONSO

These are not natural events; they strengthen
From strange to stranger. Say, how came you hither?
Boatswain
    If I did think, sir, I were well awake,
    I'ld strive to tell you. We were dead of sleep,
    And--how we know not--all clapp'd under hatches;
    Where but even now with strange and several noises
    Of roaring, shrieking, howling, jingling chains,
    And more diversity of sounds, all horrible,
    We were awaked; straightway, at liberty;
    Where we, in all her trim, freshly beheld
    Our royal, good and gallant ship, our master
    Capering to eye her: on a trice, so please you,
    Even in a dream, were we divided from them
    And were brought moping hither.
ARIEL
[Aside to PROSPERO] Was't well done?
PROSPERO
[Aside to ARIEL] Bravely, my diligence. Thou shalt be
free.
ALONSO
    This is as strange a maze as e'er men trod
    And there is in this business more than nature
    Was ever conduct of: some oracle
    Must rectify our knowledge.
PROSPERO
    Sir, my liege,
    Do not infest your mind with beating on
    The strangeness of this business; at pick'd leisure
    Which shall be shortly, single I'll resolve you,
    Which to you shall seem probable, of every
    These happen'd accidents; till when, be cheerful
    And think of each thing well.

Aside to ARIEL

Come hither, spirit:
Set Caliban and his companions free;
Untie the spell.

Exit ARIEL

How fares my gracious sir?
There are yet missing of your company
Some few odd lads that you remember not.

*Re-enter ARIEL, driving in CALIBAN, STEPHANO and
TRINCULO, in their stolen apparel*

STEPHANO
    Every man shift for all the rest, and
    let no man take care for himself; for all is
    but fortune. Coragio, bully-monster, coragio!
TRINCULO
    If these be true spies which I wear in my head,
    here's a goodly sight.
CALIBAN
    O Setebos, these be brave spirits indeed!
    How fine my master is! I am afraid
    He will chastise me.
SEBASTIAN
    Ha, ha!
    What things are these, my lord Antonio?
    Will money buy 'em?
ANTONIO
    Very like; one of them
    Is a plain fish, and, no doubt, marketable.
PROSPERO
    Mark but the badges of these men, my lords,
    Then say if they be true. This mis-shapen knave,

His mother was a witch, and one so strong
That could control the moon, make flows and ebbs,
And deal in her command without her power.
These three have robb'd me; and this demi-devil--
For he's a bastard one--had plotted with them
To take my life. Two of these fellows you
Must know and own; this thing of darkness!
Acknowledge mine.

CALIBAN

I shall be pinch'd to death.

ALONSO

Is not this Stephano, my drunken butler?

SEBASTIAN

He is drunk now: where had he wine?

ALONSO

And Trinculo is reeling ripe: where should they
Find this grand liquor that hath gilded 'em?
How camest thou in this pickle?

TRINCULO

I have been in such a pickle since I
saw you last that, I fear me, will never out of
my bones: I shall not fear fly-blowing.

SEBASTIAN

Why, how now, Stephano!

STEPHANO

O, touch me not; I am not Stephano, but a cramp.

PROSPERO

You'ld be king o' the isle, sirrah?

STEPHANO

I should have been a sore one then.

ALONSO

This is a strange thing as e'er I look'd on.

Pointing to Caliban

PROSPERO

He is as disproportion'd in his manners
As in his shape. Go, sirrah, to my cell;
Take with you your companions; as you look
To have my pardon, trim it handsomely.

CALIBAN

Ay, that I will; and I'll be wise hereafter
And seek for grace. What a thrice-double ass
Was I, to take this drunkard for a god
And worship this dull fool!

PROSPERO

Go to; away!

ALONSO

Hence, and bestow your luggage where you found it.

SEBASTIAN

Or stole it, rather.

Exeunt CALIBAN, STEPHANO, and TRINCULO

PROSPERO

Sir, I invite your highness and your train
To my poor cell, where you shall take your rest
For this one night; which, part of it, I'll waste
With such discourse as, I not doubt, shall make it
Go quick away; the story of my life
And the particular accidents gone by
Since I came to this isle: and in the morn
I'll bring you to your ship and so to Naples,
Where I have hope to see the nuptial
Of these our dear-beloved solemnized;
And thence retire me to my Milan, where
Every third thought shall be my grave.

ALONSO

I long
To hear the story of your life, which must

Take the ear strangely.
PROSPERO
I'll deliver all;
And promise you calm seas, auspicious gales
And sail so expeditious that shall catch
Your royal fleet far off.

Aside to ARIEL

My Ariel, chick,
That is thy charge: then to the elements
Be free, and fare thou well! Please you, draw near.

Exeunt

EPILOGUE

SPOKEN BY PROSPERO

Now my charms are all o'erthrown,
And what strength I have's mine own,
Which is most faint: now, 'tis true,
I must be here confined by you,
Or sent to Naples. Let me not,
Since I have my dukedom got
And pardon'd the deceiver, dwell
In this bare island by your spell;
But release me from my bands
With the help of your good hands:
Gentle breath of yours my sails
Must fill, or else my project fails,
Which was to please. Now I want
Spirits to enforce, art to enchant,
And my ending is despair,
Unless I be relieved by prayer,
Which pierces so that it assaults
Mercy itself and frees all faults.
As you from crimes would pardon'd be,
Let your indulgence set me free.

Biography

A Short Life of Edward de Vere,
17th Earl of Oxford

by Dr. Kevin Gilvary, President
The de Vere Society

He was born on 12 April 1550 at Castle
Hedingham, his family's ancestral home. His father, John
de Vere, 16th Earl, was Lord Great Chamberlain and
attended the coronations of both Mary and Elizabeth
Tudor. His mother was Margaret Golding. Edward was 11
when, in 1561, Queen Elizabeth visited Hedingham for
four days of masques, feasting and entertainments. When
his father died in 1562, young Oxford left to become, like
Bertram in *All's Well that Ends Well*, a ward of the Crown
under the guardianship of William Cecil, the Queen's
private secretary (later Lord Burghley, Lord Treasurer).
His mother married Charles Tyrrell and seems to have
passed out of the boy's life. His sister Mary went to live
with her stepfather and the siblings were not reunited for
some years.

According to a curriculum in Cecil's own hand,
Edward de Vere's daily studies included dancing, French,
Latin, writing and drawing, cosmography, penmanship,
riding, shooting, exercise and prayer. Edward de Vere
showed a prodigious talent for scholarship from his early
years, and we may ascribe his lifelong love of learning to
the influence of two of his early tutors. The first was Sir
Thomas Smith who was, perhaps, England's most
respected Greek scholar and the former Cambridge tutor
of Sir William Cecil. It was, no doubt, through Cecil's
influence that Edward de Vere spent some time living in
the household of Smith in his early years, during which

time he spent about five months at Smith's alma mater, Queens' College, Cambridge. Smith was a scholar of widely varied interests – this was reflected in his 400-volume library, some of which is still extant at Cambridge. De Vere's other tutor was Laurence Nowell, who was not only an accomplished cartographer but was also England's premier scholar of Anglo-Saxon literature – it was Nowell who possessed the only known copy of *Beowulf*.

Another important influence on Edward de Vere's early studies was his maternal uncle Arthur Golding, an officer in the Court of Wards under Cecil, who is credited with the translation of Ovid's *Metamorphoses*, published in 1567, a book widely recognised as having a major influence on 'Shakespeare'.

Following on from his matriculation at Cambridge in November 1558, Edward was awarded an honorary MA by Cambridge during a Royal progress in August 1564, and another degree by Oxford University during a Royal progress in 1566. Edward de Vere then attended Gray's Inn to study law. One notable feature of the Elizabethan Inns of Court was a tradition of mounting dramatic productions and of hosting the various touring companies of players.

In 1570 he served in a military campaign in Scotland under the Earl of Sussex. By 1571, he was reported as a leading luminary of the Court and, for a time, a favourite of Queen Elizabeth. In December 1571 he married Anne Cecil, aged 15, daughter of his guardian. This was a dynastic marriage where all the advantage accrued to Cecil who, ennobled as Baron Burghley, had reduced the social gap between himself and the young Earl.

While Oxford was away on a Grand Tour of Europe, he heard that his daughter Elizabeth Vere had been born in July 1575. On his return in early 1576, he appeared to have been convinced that Elizabeth was not his child; consequently he became estranged from Anne for five years, and exiled himself from Court, taking up residence in the Savoy and concerning himself with literary and musical patronage.

Already, in 1573, *Cardanus Comfort* (the Consolations of Boethius) had been translated from Latin by Thomas Bedingfield and dedicated to Oxford; and published with a preface written by him. In 1576 an anthology, *A Paradise of Daintie Devices*, including several poems by Oxford, was published. These are juvenile works but already show affinities, in both style and thought, with those of the mature Shakespeare.

Oxford's Grand Tour had taken in Paris, Strasbourg, Venice, Genoa, Florence, Palermo and, on his way back through France, Rousillon – the setting for *Love's Labour's Lost*. Oxford spent the best part of a year travelling in Italy in 1576, and becoming involved with moneylenders. He came back to England fluent in Italian and well acquainted with the northern Italian cities, to be satirised by Gabriel Harvey as 'The Italian Earl'. On his way back his ship was attacked by pirates in the English Channel (cf. *Hamlet*). Fourteen of 'Shakespeare's' plays have Italian settings, in which he put his detailed knowledge of the country, beyond pure book knowledge, to good use.

1573 saw the birth of Henry Wriothesley, Earl of Southampton. Although history has not bequeathed to us any evidence of a direct relationship between the two men, in the relatively small world of the royal Court, they must have been acquainted with each other. The poems *Venus and Adonis* (1593) and *The Rape of Lucrece* (1594) were dedicated to Southampton. These were the first works to be published under the name 'Shakespeare' and for the next five years the records show the byline 'Shakespeare' to have been associated exclusively with these two poems. Plays under the name 'Shakespeare' did not appear in print until 1598, the year that Lord Burghley died.

In May 1577 Oxford invested in Frobisher's voyage in the ship *Edward Bonaventure*. Despite its name, the ship's voyage across the Atlantic in search of the North-West Passage lost money; consequently he was forced to sell three estates (cf. Hamlet's words 'I am but mad north-north-west' II.1.). In 1578 he invested in Frobisher's second expedition, which also lost money, forcing further sales of estates.

He was mentioned by Gabriel Harvey in an address to Queen Elizabeth in July 1578, as a prolific private poet and one 'whose countenance shakes spears'. In the same year John Lyly, Oxford's secretary, published *Euphues.The Anatomy of Wit*, followed in 1579 by *Euphues and his England*, dedicated to Oxford. These two books launched the fashion for 'Euphuism', a style characterized by high-flown language, satirized in *Love's Labour's Lost*.

In March 1581 Oxford's mistress, Anne Vavasour, who was one of Queen Elizabeth's Ladies of the Bedchamber, gave birth to a son. The lovers and their son were sent to the Tower by an infuriated Queen but swiftly released (cf. *Measure for Measure*). After his release, Oxford was wounded in a street-fight provoked by Thomas Knyvet, a kinsman of Anne Vavasour; affrays continued in the streets of London between the rival gangs of supporters for over a year (cf.*Romeo and Juliet*).

In December 1581 he resumed living with his long-suffering and devoted wife, and accepted Elizabeth Vere as his child. Tragically, their only son died one day after his birth. Three more daughters followed, of whom Susan and Bridget survived.

In 1584, Robert Greene's *Gwydonius; the Card of Fancy* was dedicated to him, identifying him as a 'preeminent writer'. In 1586, when he was 36, he served on the tribunal which condemned Mary, Queen of Scots to execution.

In the same year, the Queen awarded Oxford an unconditional pension of £1,000 a year for life (about £500,000 at today's value). The motive for this uncharacteristic generosity on the part of the Queen remains a mystery – no accounting was required of Oxford. Her successor, King James I, continued to pay the pension. In reply to Sir Robert Cecil's request that Lord Sheffield's pension be increased, the King refused, saying, 'Great Oxford got no more . . .', leaving us to wonder why Great Oxford? His greatness does not seem to have resided in war or any of the known offices of State. Perhaps a clue can be found in a letter to Burghley, written in 1594, in which Edward de Vere seeks his favour in a matter involving what he describes as 'in mine office' and that this office is beholden to the Queen.

In 1589, George Puttenham published *The Arte of English Poesie* and this contains the most telling recognition of Edward de Vere's literary standing amongst his contemporaries: 'And in her Majesties time that now is are sprong up an other crew of Courtly makers Noble men and Gentlemen of her Majesties owne servantes, who have written excellently well as it would appeare if their doings could be found out and made publicke with the rest, of which number is first that noble Gentleman Edward Earle of Oxford.'

In 1588 his wife Anne, daughter of Lord Burghley, died and in extant letters written at this time, it is reported that Burghley is so incapacitated by grief over the death of his favourite daughter that he is incapable of conducting any Privy Council business.

Three years later, in 1591, Oxford married another of the Queen's Maids of Honour, Elizabeth Trentham, with whom he finally became the father of a male heir;

Henry de Vere, 18th Earl of Oxford. Although there is evidence of his continued involvement in Court affairs, from the date of this marriage Edward de Vere's life at his new home at King's Place in Hackney is perhaps the most obscure of his entire life.

In 1594, his ship the *Edward Bonaventure* was wrecked in Bermuda (cf. *The Tempest*). In January 1595, Elizabeth Vere married William Stanley, 6th Earl of Derby, another literary earl who maintained his own company of players – many scholars believe that *A Midsummer Night's Dream* was written for these festivities which were attended by the whole royal Court.

On September 7 1598, Francis Meres' *Palladis Tamia* was registered for publication, naming Oxford as the 'best for comedy'. This is a vital document in Shakespearean history because it includes the first mention of 'Shakespeare' as a playwright, attributing twelve plays to him; until then Shakespeare's reputation had rested on the two narrative poems only.

Oxford suffered all his life from financial difficulties, much of which can be traced to the fact that Queen Elizabeth handed out the bulk of his estate to her favourite courtier the Earl of Leicester during Oxford's minority as a royal ward (estates which Oxford found almost impossible to reclaim), and the ruinous debt she placed upon him over his marriage to Anne Cecil. It is, however, notable that his new brother-in-law, the wealthy Staffordshire landowner and Knight of the Shire Francis Trentham, took over the management of Edward de Vere's near-bankrupt estate from 1591 and gradually nursed it back to health so that, when Oxford died, all of his massive debts had been cleared.

On the Queen's death in 1603 Oxford wrote eloquently to Sir Robert Cecil, son and heir of Lord Burghley, of his 'great grief'. He wrote, 'In this common shipwreck, mine is above all the rest, who least regarded, though often comforted, she hath left to try my fortune among the alterations of time and chance'.

Oxford died in Hackney in 1604, cause unknown. Parish records state that he was buried in Hackney Church on July 6, but a family history by his first cousin Percival Golding, states 'Edward de Veer ... a man in mind and body absolutely accomplished with honorable endowments ... lieth buried at Westminster'. No record of such a burial can now be traced in Westminster Abbey, where there is a Vere family tomb.

The Aftermath of Oxford's life and death

During the winter season 1604-05, six of Shakespeare's plays were presented at Court by command of King James I. This has an air of commemoration. In 1609 the *Sonnets* were published in a pirated edition. The famous dedication describes the author as 'our ever-living', a phrase invariably used only of the dead.

In 1622 Henry Peacham published, in *The Compleat Gentelman*, a list of poets who made Elizabeth's reign a 'golden age'. Unaccountably, he omitted Shakespeare but placed the Earl of Oxford in first place in his list – perhaps he knew them to be the same person. This is unlike Meres who included them both – maybe one reason was because he didn't know Oxford and Shakespeare were the same person.

We do not know who instigated publication of the First Folio Edition of the Shakespeare plays in 1623, but there is no mention of any executor or relative of Shakspere of Stratford in connection with it. However, of the two brothers who financed it and to whom it was dedicated, one – Philip Earl of Montgomery – was the husband of Oxford's daughter Susan, while the other – William Earl of Pembroke – had once been a suitor for her sister Bridget. Pembroke was Lord Chamberlain, the supreme authority in the world of theatre, and thus in a position to decide which plays were to be published and which suppressed. We also know that Ben Jonson, who wrote much of the introductory material, was an intimate associate of the de Vere family after Oxford's death. The First Folio was therefore very much a family affair, but the family was not the one in Stratford-on-Avon.

An AfterVerse

For those with yet an interest
In strenuous debate
We've compiled a list of books and films
Your appetite to sate.
From this study clear your mind
Of doubt and all misgiving-
Who from us has long since gone
And who is ever-living.

Selected References & Bibliography
About the Author
Edward de Vere, 17th Earl of Oxford

Books

♦ Anderson, M. (2005). *Shakespeare by Another Name: The Life of Edward de Vere, Earl of Oxford, The Man who was Shakespeare.* New York: Gotham Books.
--A physicist by training with research interest in how evidence supports or negates a theory, Mark Anderson spent ten years investigating Edward de Vere as the author of Shake-speare's works.

♦Farina, William. (2006). *De Vere as Shakespeare: An Oxfordian Reading of the Canon.*
Jefferson, NC. McFarland & Company.
--Each of the plays and poems is individually assessed

and explored in its own chapter, using the innumerable connections between the text itself and the life of its author, Edward de Vere.

♦ Looney, J. Thomas (2018). *Shakespeare Identified.* Cary, N.C. Veritas Publicaations.
--First published in 1920 this book began the modern Oxfordian movement. From reading it, Sigmund Freud became convinced and John Galsworthy called it "the best detective story I ever read."

♦ Ogburn, C. (1992). *The Mysterious William Shakespeare.* McLean (Va.): EPM.
--An in depth exploration and must read foundational book on the authorship question.

♦Sobran, Joseph. (1997). *Alias Shakespeare: Solving the Greatest Literary Mystery of All Time.* New York; The Free Press, A Division of Simon & Schuster.
--A concise exploration of the puzzling questions surrounding the authorship controversy with the evidence decisively supporting the case for Edward de Vere, the 17th Earl of Oxford, as the rightful author of the Shakespeare plays and poems.

♦Whittemore, Hank. (2016), *100 Reasons Shake-speare Was the Earl of Oxford.* Somerville MA. Forever Press.
►Also with further discussion and public comment at:
Hank Whittemore's Shakespeare Blog.
   https://hankwhittemore.com/
--In both the book and online blog cited above,

Whittemore presents a concise introduction to the authorship question that examines 100 different aspects, from biographical and historical records, that point to Edward de Vere as the true writer of the Shake-speare plays and poems.

Websites & Videos

▶ De Vere Society. (2019). The de Vere Society – Dedicated to the proposition that the works of Shakespeare were written by Edward de Vere, 17th Earl of Oxford. [online] Deveresociety.co.uk. Available at: https://deveresociety.co.uk
--A very complete resource with substantial biographical and authorship information and links.

▶ The Oxford Fellowship (2019). Shakespeare Oxford Fellowship | Research and Discussion of the Shakespeare Authorship Question. [online] Shakespeare Oxford Fellowship. Available at: https://shakespeareoxfordfellowship.org/
--A seminal online resource especially focusing on the authorship question.

▶ Waugh, A. (2019). Alexander Waugh. [online] YouTube. Available at: https://www.youtube.com/channel/UCHN7SCKlsa9l PYJmqqQ2uIg/featured/
OR simply search: 'Alexander Waugh'
--Alexander Waugh is a leading authorship scholar who has produced many fascinating video presentations on the authorship question. This link is to his YouTube Channel.

► Columbia Pictures & Centropolis Entertainment. (2011). *Anonymous.* Produced and directed by Roland Emmerich. [DVD]
--This mainstream film is both entertaining and enlightening. It presents a superb dramatization of the character of Edward de Vere, setting out in detail the historical and personal context which made his anonymous authorship necessary.

►Centropolis Entertainment and First Folio Pictures. *Last Will and Testament.* (2012). [DVD]
--A thoughtful and ground-breaking video documentary introduction to the Shakespeare authorship question.

Acknowledgment
Our sincere thanks to
The de Vere Society
and
The Shakespeare Oxford Fellowship
*for their inspiration, help and support
in creating this series.*

Attributions
*--Character list from Wikipedia under
the Creative Commons License 3.0
--Play text from the Moby(tm) editions
in the public domain*

Photos
Coat of Arms of Edward de Vere
Source: Wikimedia.org
Author: George Baker / Public domain

The Keep at Castle Hedingham
Source: geograph.org.uk
Author: David Phillips / CC BY-SA 2.0

The de Vere Family Coat of Arms
Source: Wikimedia
Author: Rs-nourse / CC BY-SA 3.0
(https://creativecommons.org/licenses/by-sa/3.0)

View from The Minstrels' Gallery, Hedingham Castle
Source: geograph.org.uk/p/3162585
Photo by: © PAUL FARMER – cc-by-sa/2.0

Cover/Inside: The Welbeck portrait of Edward de Vere (1575).
Artist unknown. National Portrait Gallery, London.

This work has been edited and produced by

Verus Publishing
www.verusbooks.com

V | P